HOW TO PLAY THE FIDDLE.

OR

HINTS TO BEGINNERS ON THE VIOLIN.

BY

HENRY WILLIAM GRESSWELL, M.A., Oxon.

AND

GEORGE GRESSWELL, B.A., Oxon.

"In all things we can do something at first. Any man will forge a bar of iron if you give him a hammer—not so well as a smith but tolerably; and make a box, though a clumsy one; but give him a fiddle and a fiddle-stick, and he can do nothing."—Dr. Johnson.

New Edition, Revised and Corrected.

LONDON:
W. REEVES, 83, CHARING CROSS ROAD, W.C.
1908.

SEVENTH EDITION

In the interest of creating a more extensive selection of rare historical book reprints, we have chosen to reproduce this title even though it may possibly have occasional imperfections such as missing and blurred pages, missing text, poor pictures, markings, dark backgrounds and other reproduction issues beyond our control. Because this work is culturally important, we have made it available as a part of our commitment to protecting, preserving and promoting the world's literature. Thank you for your understanding.

TO

DR. JOSEPH JOACHIM.

The greatest master of violin playing the world has ever seen.

This little work is herewith most gratefully inscribed in accordance with very gracious permission, as a tribute of esteem and veneration

BY

TWO OUT OF THE INNUMERABLE CROWD OF HIS ADMIRERS

Who, when they sought this boon, now conferred upon them by him, presumed so far, nowise because they thought the book they had written possessed in itself worth sufficient to make it rated at so great a value, but because they did believe they had in some small degree helped onwards one of the most wonderful, beautiful, and soul inspiring of all the arts, and that, in so far as they had worked for this end, they had laboured for a cause which the most renowned genius among violinists had very deeply at heart, and that the task they had undertaken, even if it attained only a small measure of success, would yet please a man who by his inimitable and perfect skill has so largely increased the sum of human happiness, by elevating the minds of thousands and thousands of his fellow-creatures to heights of pleasure, and ambition, and delight in the consciousness of man's well-nigh illimitable power for good to heights of rapture perhaps before unknown and undreamt of.

PREFACE TO THE FIRST EDITION.

In this little work it is hoped there will be found some hints, which may be useful to those who are about to learn violin playing. In the present day, when the desire to acquire this accomplishment is certainly becoming more general than it has hitherto been, especially among the members of the fair and gentle sex, it is well that some preliminary advice should be given, and a helping hand held out to beginners. It is also important that they, too, should seriously consider the many difficulties with which they will have to grapple, before they can become proficient in their knowledge of the fiddle.

Dr. Johnson, alluding to the special skill requisite for good violin-playing, has remarked that a novice can to some extent manage to do many things tolerably, if only he is supplied with the requisite materials; "but," said he, "give a man a fiddle and a fiddle-stick, and he can do nothing."

Let the learner, however, not be discouraged by the arduous nature of the task he has selected.

"To be forewarned is to be forearmed," and a previou knowledge of the subtle intricacies of the most perfect and most difficult musical instrument, will act rather by way of encouragement than by way of discouragement, to those who really desire to excel in playing it. Several books have been written on violin-playing: but never, so far as we are aware, has there been an attempt made to place simply clearly and concisely before the learner, the many little details which it is necessary to know at the outset. Much time and trouble, much vexation and disgust, might be saved, if such apparently trivial matters were attended to as soon as possible. A pupil of Michael Angelo, thinking that his master, by a few bold strokes, could fashion out his clay, when he observed him spending much time on details, remarked, "Why waste your time on trifles?" "Success is made up of trifles, and success is no trifle," replied the master. The same applies not only to sculpture, but to everything—to music, painting, writing, walking, reading, and, in short, to all vital actions. It may be said that it is just the concentrated attention to all parts of a subject needed for perfection, which marks the successful man. How many there are who fail through carelessness in *little* points! Especially is it true that those who wish to play the violin even fairly, must concentrate their attention on a multiplicity of small but very important points. If the pupil neglects to observe these details at the outset, he will find to his cost and vexation, that he has lost a great deal of time; and he will be obliged to go over again, and with the greatest care, the ground which he has already trod. Starting afresh is always more arduous than the original beginning; for, in addition to the difficulty of studying what ought to have been learnt at first, one has also to unlearn what one has learnt wrongly. Habits once formed are abandoned only with a struggle.

However irksome attention to little matters may be, the student will, when in course of time the power of playing tolerably has been acquired, have no reason to regret that a considerable amount of time and trouble was spent in mastering the intricacies of violin-playing. Let the beginner remember that "what is worth doing at all, is worth doing well." It may be said that the chief difference between different people lies in the fact, that while some endeavour to do as well as it possibly can be done, each thing they take in hand, others do badly, carelessly, and lazily, whatever they set themselves to carry out. In the case of the former, in order to ensure a successful career, the only thing requisite is to select what they like best, and therefore, as a rule, can do best; while, with regard to the latter, one may observe that, by trying to save themselves trouble, they simply increase and multiply the obstacles, which beset them on all sides. Continued efforts of will can, however, effect much, and it is undoubtedly possible largely to remedy and alter one's natural constitution.

An enduring and ever-present consciousness of the homely and well-worn proverb, that "a stitch in time saves nine," would prevent all men making many great mistakes. To ensure that our children shall be definite, precise, business-like, painstaking, and exact, should be our first aim in educating them. The formation of bad and careless habits is the chief tendency to be avoided in the pursuit of all arts and sciences—in violin-playing as in life at large. If a lazy, careless, and defective mode of working is pursued, every undertaking becomes ten times as difficult. The object should be in all cases ultimately to achieve perfection and success. Carlyle says, "Habit is our primal fundamental law;" and Dryden tells us that—

"All habits gather by unseen degrees,
As brooks made rivers, rivers run to seas."

Hence those who wish to play the fiddle well, must at the outset procure a good tutor, a good violin, and a good bow, and above all things they must make up their minds to work very hard indeed. If we aim at perfection, our ideal may not be reached, but nevertheless we shall rise to a far higher level than those to whom mediocrity is a guiding-star.

In reading, in writing, in public speaking, in acting, allowance is made for a comparatively large number of mistakes. In music, excellence is looked for. With regard to violin-playing especially, perfection is exceedingly difficult of attainment. The violin may be regarded as the queen of musical instruments, and as a sovereign who will by no means allow herself to be trifled with.

LOUTH, LINCOLNSHIRE,
    1886.

PREFACE TO THE SECOND EDITION.

As a rule, perhaps, it may be true that readers do not care a great deal about prefaces; and yet we should seem something ungrateful in our own eyes, and many others, too, might think it strange, if, now in the time of our excusable self-congratulation at this re-issue of our little book, we abstained from saying just a few words by way of thankfulness, more directly than in the pages which follow, to our kind and indulgent friends, the public. If, then, all those who are impatient of introductory observations will pass on to the body of this our work, we will linger a little while with those who will listen to us, and bear with us for a moment or two, as we try to tell them at once how thankful we are for past favours, while being hopeful of even greater things for the future. Hence, we may as well say, we hope without incurring any charge of undue exultation, that, inasmuch as ' How to Play the Fiddle " may be said to have passed a searching examination, not without high honours, as events have proved, it has thereby gained some right to rank among the more permanent literature belonging to the subject of which it treats. Consequently, we have every hope that, all being well, we shall be able to improve it more and more as years roll on, and we need scarcely say how glad we shall always be to hear any suggestions in regard to it, whenever made, and from whatsoever quarter.

The audience to whom we are now addressing ourselves will not, probably, think any the worse either of us, or of our book, when we say that our "Hints to Beginners on the Violin" were not drawn up and put together without a considerable amount of care and painstaking trouble. So much, indeed, was this the case that when we had actually decided to rush into print, and submit our treasured MS. to the fiery ordeal of public criticism, we felt justified in adopting a more courageous and taking title than the rather unpretentious one which now stands as an alternative, or secondary designation. We felt that, although we might by so doing, offend some few of those who could fully realise the difficulty of the task we had set ourselves, nevertheless we should by the implied confidence in the result of our labours please the great mass of the public, which, though it hates anything approaching to arrogance and conceit, is always most ready, and even eager to applaud honest belief in themselves on the part of new, and as yet, comparatively unknown writers. Now, we had worked hard, and we thought we had turned out a good book, and hence we felt that we might use the more emphatic title, and so we used, so to speak, a rather large quantity of sealing-wax, and made as deep an impress upon it as we could find ready to our hands.

Speaking generally, it is a very easy matter to read a book, and, as a rule, the better the book, the easier it is for a patient reader to get at the meaning expressed in each and every sentence. On the other hand it is an excessively difficult thing to write a book which is at once useful, and at the same time in some degree pleasing and entertaining in its style. We may, then, perhaps be excused if now for once we point out that such a task as the one we have selected is not justly to be likened unto those boundless sources of bliss and easy enjoyment whereof dim visions are wont to rise up in the mind, when one describes an occupation as being "all beer and skittles." We have always held that a writer should be candid, just as some most estimable persons are nothing if not critical, just as, too, a preface is not at all likely to be read if it is not seasoned with something of amusement, as well as with something of more lasting value. We cannot say how other authors manage these things, though we suspect that many of our fellow-labourers are not unlike ourselves in these matters; but at any rate we, for our part, feel that, like honest Dogberry, we may justly claim some right to the honours conferred upon respectability; for true it most certainly is that, in common with that authority and with very many of the children of prosperity, we have had losses. It is some consolation, as Sir Walter Scott points out, to all who are like us in this respect, that a loss manifestly implies the previous possession of something to lose. Not only did it seem to us that we had lost some time and trouble, some self-reliance, and not a little of that most desirable human sentiment called hope, but we had suffered a still more pressingly inconvenient loss, a loss namely of money, which despise it as men may, must none the less be looked upon as a very needful possession, particularly in these days. Well! perchance we are on the verge of finding that our seeming losses will in the long run turn out to be losses merely in appearance, and in reality gains. In point of fact the publication of our first edition was at once a success, and yet a failure from a pecuniary point of view. Although the thousand copies printed were all disposed of within a period of a little more than a year following "its first appearance on any stage," and though our effort was so far successful as to meet with a great deal of praise, and was assailed with no adverse criticism, so far as we know, still the sale did not at first appear to promise so well as to justify the additional expense which would have been incurred if the type had been kept up. The result was that what with printing and advertisements and corrections of proofs, and so on, we ourselves had lost a a sum not to be despised, as times go; and moreover, to our great sorrow and dismay, we learnt that even the publishers of that edition had not been so very much more lucky than we had been, they also being slightly out of pocket by the transaction. Now this was not at all what we had anticipated; for, though we had not supposed ourselves or our book capable of setting the Thames on fire, we certainly had hoped for better things from the financial point of view. Here, then, was a case in which, although authors, printers, publishers, booksellers, and last, but very far from least, reviewers, had all done their best, still, notwithstanding a certain and rather

PREFACE TO THE SECOND EDITION.

large amount of encouragement from the public, losses of actual cash out of pocket, not to speak of much time and labour of many and various kinds, had been sustained. The hasty judge might say "Oh! the book itself was not sufficiently good, or, if good, perhaps it was not wanted." That this could not possibly be the case, the present peremptory, not to say impatient, demand on the part of the public furnishes sufficient proof. As a matter of fact the causes of the difficulties encountered in bringing any book, however good it may be, into favour, are very deeply seated and numerous; and it may be added that a somewhat lengthened period must in every case elapse, before the result can be said to be final. Even that noted novel, "Called Back," is said to have fallen flat at first. However this may be, we at least are not above confessing that at one time we had well-nigh lost our pristine confident ambition that "How to play the Fiddle," despite its perhaps something too bold title, would appear upon the boards, or rather in the shops, again, eager for the public ear. Yet so it has turned out, though in a manner that was quite unforeseen by us: and, now that our tiny bark sets sail from port once more, blown by very favourable winds into seas which look propitious, and backed up by some esteem at the hands of an indulgent and kind public, not without a deep sense of gratefulness from ourselves—now, once more :—

"Hope, bright Hope directs her eye,
To some clear spot just breaking in the sky"—

now, once more, it is incumbent upon us to express in fitting words, if by good luck our pen can find them, the pleasure we feel in bowing ourselves, as a preliminary to telling our gentle readers, as best we can, how to fiddle with the best and easiest grace, how to bow in the most approved manner. We do not pretend to brilliant success; but we do lay claim to having provided a useful aid to beginners.

The fact is that literary success must be a thing of slow and gradual growth in any times, and especially, of course, in these days when the competition is so excessive. Even authors who seem to have jumped into fame at one bold stroke, have not really done so; and, if those few persons who are envious of the laurels that have been gained, could form any adequate conception of the amount of toil and labour and sinking of the heart which have in at least ninety-nine cases out of every hundred preceded the victory so long delayed, they might perhaps concentrate their jealousy on other forms of glory, but certainly not on that achieved by the craftsmen of the quill. We just cite the case of "How to play the Fiddle" as one instance out of very many which could be mentioned, in which the publication of a book, which afterwards proves to have supplied a real want, is by no means a direct and immediate benefit either to the author or to the publisher. It is in short a task of great magnitude in these days, or in fact, in any days, to write in such a manner as to ensure one's rising from the honourable but arduous position of a struggling author, with whom, in truth, but few sympathise, into the bright halo and brilliant and dazzling glory of the well-known writer, whose name is bandied about after the manner of a shuttlecock, shall we say?—with something of respect and a great deal of curiosity from mouth to mouth by means of the battledore of public opinion. For a long time the public is cautious and even suspicious, and the new candidate for a small portion of the "popularis aura" must humble himself or herself, and possess her or his soul in patience. She or he must, if need be, develop a spirit of stolidity, and perhaps even of indifference to those buffets with which the fickle jade, the wanton and tantalising tormentor, pretty mistress Fortune, is sure to bow him or her down for a protracted season, and it may be that the mind will be occasionally overcome with despondency or even despair, and sometimes revert to those wondering words of Hamlet:—

> "To be, or not to be, that is the question:
> Whether 'tis nobler in the mind to suffer
> The slings and arrows of outrageous fortune;
> Or to take up arms against a sea of troubles,
> And, by opposing, end them?"—

If there is one thing which is needed more than another to ensure literary success, it is that determined will, that indomitable resolution, that elasticity of spirit, which, though it may not enable its possessor to smile when the world frowns, will at least incite to redoubled efforts. Then, *if things be well*, the courageous persistence will at last be crowned with laurels and more substantial rewards—if not well, the worker will at least be conscious of some consolation, some soothing balm, in that the battle has not been lost without a grim struggle. All this may seem a little off the point; but the lesson we are trying to teach applies not only to writers and writings, but also to all the numerous and varied kinds of activity which are known among men. Violinists, no less than writers, must wade through a heavy sea of difficulties, must pick their way o'er flood and fell and crag, ay! and over huge mountains too! if they are any wise desirous of shining out in excellence before the world.

Arguments based upon seeming analogies are apt to be misleading; but we may at least point out that beginners of all kinds, violinists no less than writers of books, are, at least at the outset of their career, and also, though to a far less extent during the whole course of it, almost absolutely dependent upon the opinions of a *few*, and we may add that very possibly these few may not be good and competent, even if they are fair and righteous judges. Hence it happens—and in the long run in the average of cases it is best that it does so happen—that only by dint of the most incessant, prolonged, and strenuous, exertions, can any beginner prove the possession of skill and talent. It is not of much use to tell would-be authors that they must not think of having a book printed unless they can find a publisher who will undertake the sole expense of it. Indeed, this would not even be good advice to give. Similarly, it would be very stupid indeed for a violinist who has not proved his or her attainments to expect to receive large rewards at first. Just as the writer, having regard to the great initial difficulties with which the profession is replete, must serve a long apprenticeship, ay! and pay rather heavily for his articles, too, so also the violinist must be content to work for nothing for a considerable period of time, before some degree of success has been achieved.

PREFACE TO THE SECOND EDITION.

The author of a good work may offer his book for a five-pound-note, simply because of an anxious desire to give it a chance to meet the public eye; he or she might even go so far as to express a wish to give it to a publisher, if he will but bring it out at his own expense; and, as likely as not, if the writer is as yet unknown, the offer will be categorically refused. What is to be done? What can be done? Nothing, absolutely nothing, unless, indeed, the writer has the means to pay for the printing and publishing of the book written, or can spare the time which would be necessary for re-writing it thoroughly from end to end, and for submitting it for consideration to publisher after publisher again and again, and yet again, and again, and again. Even then failure, and not success may crown every effort, failure—mark you, which, after all, may not be due to faults in the work itself. However, not only is it true that these things cannot be helped, but on the average it is undeniable that they are better so. As it is, some bad books are brought before the public, and on the other hand, anyone who can form a true conception of the great difficulties which the beginner has to contend with, would at least admit the possibility that some good works are never produced at all. So far as the world at large is concerned, this does not matter very much; for it is troubled with a surfeit of literature, rather than with a deficiency. At least one very important conclusion will occur to us, if we pay due regard to these and similar facts, and that is, that no needy person should take up the vocation of a writer, except as an aid to other means of subsistence, unless, indeed, the road sketched out is known to be a pretty safe one for the wayfarer in question. In every age the practice of writing has been looked up to, and justly so, and furthermore it has always been considered to be a better aid to progression in the case of those who do not need its help, than it is in the case of those who are actually dependent upon it.

In other words, as has been often said, literature may indeed furnish a pretty good stick; but it is a very bad crutch. Writing, and painting, and violin-playing, the composition of music, songs, or plays, the calling of the sculptor and the carver, are all alike, in one respect; and that is, that excellence is looked for in these pursuits, and the penalties exacted from those who do not surpass their brethren are oftentimes severe. The reason of this is, that the very best work can only be evoked by sustained and almost gigantic labour; and there are but few men and women who are capable of the self-denial and concentration which is necessary, unless there is some rigorous compulsion threatening them in the not far distant background of dismal and ghastly failure. All men and women fear and fly away from failure and ruin; and especially do those persons dread obscurity who can fully realise that the battle is not always to the strong nor the race always to the swift. There is on every side something which reminds human beings of the terrible uncertainty of all men's doings, and it is particularly those who see this weird uncertainty most clearly who will submit to almost every possible inconvenience rather than fail, and who consequently achieve those mighty deeds which men wonder at, while they applaud them. If we enquire into the conditions under which the greatest works have been done in the world, we shall often find that obstacles, which seemed well-nigh insurmountable, were by no means the smallest of the factors which led to the strenuous efforts, wherewith alone those works could have been produced. Nevertheless, while we admit fully that any lessening of the difficulties of attaining success in the world would probably lead to a deterioration in the quality of men's achievements, it cannot but seem very hard indeed on those who never have the initial chances; for it must always be remembered that, though the world at large is a very excellent and just judge of the men and women in it, and of their deeds whether good, bad, or indifferent, still it is very generally true that individuals and even isolated groups of individuals are apt to be very bad and often very unfair judges indeed. Hence it happens that a thing which is exceptionally good is often more likely to be rejected, than is a work (poem, book, play, or what not) which, though it accords with the established routine, and breaks no important rules, is yet in its essence, if not worthless, at least of mediocre quality, and possessed of

PREFACE TO THE SECOND EDITION.

but little depth and power. This train of thought reminds one of those oft-quoted lines of the poet of all time:—

> "Authority intoxicates;
> The fumes of it invade the brain
> And make men giddy, proud, and vain.
> By this the fool commands the wise,
> The noble with the base complies;
> The sot assumes the rule of wit,
> And cowards make the brave submit."

This, however, is nothing like so true as it used to be. The world is becoming more fair, more just, more charitable. False and despotic kinds of power, though doubtless they still exist all over the world, are fast becoming looked upon as anachronisms indicative of conditions of a barbarism now fast disappearing. So far from repining at what is wrong around us, let us, therefore, look to the brighter side of the picture presented to our view. The world, taking it as a whole, might be very much worse, much more cruel, though indeed, it is very cruel still. Especially ought all those of us who are practically safe to try to lessen the misery which still exists so largely in our midst. There are many, many ways in which men, and women, and children, may be made far happier than they are. Some may say, "The world is best as it is: let us not try to tinker, or tamper with, the laws of human life." We cannot admit this contention for a moment, and those who are charitably minded will agree with us that there is a great deal of room for charity, for compassion, for help, especially among those unhappy ones who are doomed to live in want for all their lives, among those for whom Ruskin and Besant and many other able writers have written, again and again. We should like to see a great deal more voluntary help of a substantial and enduring kind held out to those who cannot greatly help themselves, strive as they may.

We have travelled away from our point, for the misery we have been alluding to has little or nothing to do with either writing or violin-playing, as we understand those pursuits, except in so far as it bears upon the general question of the hotly-contested struggle which is ever going on in human life at large, and of the difficulties of attaining any measure of success in any department of work whatsoever. The reason why we started this discussion was that we might perhaps do something towards showing how arduous a thing is literary advancement, and how thankful one ought to be for any step upwards on the ladder of popular goodwill. There can be no harm in pointing out the nature of some few of the obstacles which oppose themselves to the gaining of any position of eminence among men of letters.

Now, with regard to the way in which our little book was received, we feel that our very best thanks are due to all those ladies and gentlemen—for we certainly think we may number some members of the fair sex, both among our readers and among our critics—who have spoken in favourable or eulogistic terms of our attempt to provide the public with a book we felt to be greatly needed, one of instruction and of help to amateur fiddlers. We had always heard that reviewers are as a rule very chary of their much-prized and eagerly searched-for favours, and it is certain that sometimes they will, by way of discouragement, as it seems, wax satirical, and even do what may possibly be even a worse thing for a book than give it an unfavourable notice. We, however, have not found this to be the case, and we are thankful to be able to say so.

We repeat, then, that we feel we have much to be grateful for, at the hands of that mighty engine of civilisation, the press, and especially at the hands of our *puissant*, but kind judges, the critics, to whose good efforts on our behalf we in chief part owe the fact that we have been able to make a second appearance before the public in the capacity of authors of "How to Play the Fiddle." It is our earnest hope that the book in its new dress and improved form will not fail to elicit cries of "encore" from all old and new friends and lovers of the violin, into whose hands it may chance to fall.

Many mighty engines of public opinion have pronounced a favourable verdict on our humble effort, and to those unknown benefactors we are all the more thankful, perhaps, because we know their good gifts were freely given to us in a spirit of fair play and appreciation of the book for the book's sake. Nevertheless, as we have said, we have had losses, and certain it is that we should have been more mirthful and joyous and light-hearted, if instead of being touched in the region of a rather tender corn, we had gained a little wholesome coin of our good Queen's realm to line our pockets withal. Touch a man's pocket, especially if it be nearly empty to begin with, and you are bound to make him wince in no measured degree. The pocket is a very tender part of a man's belongings, giving rise to much mental pain when tapped.

All that was over, and our countenances, somewhat downcast at the time, received some almost forgotten touches of rejoicing, when Mr. William Reeves, of 185, Fleet Street, London, the well-known and highly-esteemed publisher, made a proposal to us which surprised us no less than it pleased us. By the mouth of one of his representatives, he offered to reprint and re-publish our little work at his own expense, and give us half his profits, after his outlay had been recouped. The book was then out of print: hence to Mr. Reeves belongs all the credit which may attach itself to the production of this second edition of "How to Play the Fiddle." At that time our minds, having gone through many phases of thought about the book, were somewhat in the condition of the heart which is sickened with hope deferred; and no words are adequate to describe the excess of joyfulness, and the bright visions of success which the offer of Mr. Reeves implied. It was like the cup of water held out to the lips of the weary traveller who is well nigh sinking in the desert.

Just another word or two we add in this year of rejoicing for all who love Great Britain and our noble Queen. There are divisions of time which may seem in themselves something arbitrary; but that day which marks a climax of fifty years' most righteous ruling over our glorious Empire should be recognised by each and all of us as one of the most profound importance. It is at such periods of sacred jubilation, that the love that her loyal subjects bear her can be most

PREFACE TO THE SECOND EDITION

fittingly expressed, and made manifest in truest homage to our gracious and mighty Empress of the seas. It is at such times that Britons should try to realise in the fulness of its deep significance that theirs is the greatest Kingdom which the world has ever seen, and that they have indeed been blessed in the wise and gentle sway of the sceptre for half a century by her of whom one of the greatest of our living poets has spoken :—

> "Thee, mother, thee, our Queen who givest
> Assurance to the heavens most high
> And earth whereon her bondsmen sigh
> That by the sea's grace while thou livest
> Hope shall not wholly die."
>
> SWINBURNE.

This, our work, appears now at this most auspicious season of joyfulness, and we feel that our remarks may therefore suitably close with two more beautiful verses taken from Algernon Charles Swinburne's poem, which is doubtless flying all over to the uttermost parts of the wide earth, to east and west and south and north.

> "Hope, wide of eye and wild of wing,
> Rose with the sundawn of a reign
> Whose grace should make the rough ways plain,
> And fill the worn old world with spring,
> And heal its heart of pain.
> The sea, divine as heaven, and deathless,
> Is hers, and none but only she
> Hath learnt the sea's word none but we,
> Her children, hear in heart the breathless
> Bright watchword of the sea."

May we, in conclusion, hope that many will strive to enable themselves to bring domestic felicity into the households of Great Britain, and into the hearts of our people, and to enliven many a jolly group of young men and maidens, by learning how to play the fiddle. May we trust that our little attempt to scatter the seeds of happiness over the Empire may not be a fruitless one in this year of Her Most Gracious Majesty's gentle and generous supremacy.

Kelsey House, Louth, Lincolnshire

Monday, *June 6th*, 1887.

CONTENTS.

	PAGE
PREFACE to First Edition	viii. to x.
,, to Second Edition...	xi. to xxii.

CHAPTER I.

GENERAL AND INTRODUCTORY	1 to 11
A. On teaching the Violin	1
B. On Instruction-books	6
C. On Practice	8

CHAPTER II.

RELATING TO THE PURCHASE OF A VIOLIN ...	11 to 26
A. Importance of buying a Good One ...	11
B. How to set about securing a Good Violin	13
C. The Merits of Old Fiddles. Age and Use	16
D. The testing or making trial of a Fiddle	21

CHAPTER III.

| THE PRESERVATION AND REPAIR OF VIOLINS... | 26 to 29 |

CHAPTER IV.

GENERAL AND HISTORICAL	29 to 40
A. A Few Short Remarks of a General Character	29
B. A Short History of Some Celebrated Violin-makers	32

CHAPTER V.

DIFFERENT PARTS AND ADJUNCTS OF A VIOLIN	40 to 46
A. The Sound-bar and the Sound-post ...	40
B. The Bridge	42
C. A Few Words on the Pegs, the Mute, the Resin, and the Finger-board	44

CONTENTS.

CHAPTER VI.
PAGE

THE STRINGS AND THE METHOD OF ADJUSTING THEM
PROPERLY ... ... 46 to 52
  A. The Strings 46
  B. The Mode of Stringing 50

CHAPTER VII.

THE BOW AND THE MODE OF USING IT ... 53 to 61
  A. The Bow 53
  B. Bowing 57

CHAPTER VIII.

THE METHOD OF TUNING THE VIOLIN ... 62 to 67

CHAPTER IX.

SOME RULES TO BE OBSERVED IN PLAYING ... 67 to 78

CHAPTER X.

DOUBLE-STOPS, HARMONICS, SHIFTS, AND THE SHAKE 79 to 84
  A. Double-stopping 79
  B. Harmonics 80
  C. Remarks on the Shift 81
  D. The Shake 83

CHAPTER XI.

ON PLAYING WITH AN ACCOMPANIMENT ... 85 to 92

CHAPTER XII.

CONCLUDING OBSERVATIONS ... ... 92 to 100

HOW TO PLAY THE FIDDLE.

CHAPTER I.

INTRODUCTORY.

"Nothing so difficult as a beginning."—BYRON

A. ON TEACHING THE VIOLIN.

"A teacher should not be continually thundering instruction into the ears of his pupil, as if he were pouring it through a funnel; but, after having put the lad, like a young horse on a trot before him, to observe his paces, and see what he is able to perform, should, according to the extent of his capacity, induce him to taste, to distinguish, and find out things for himself, sometimes opening the way, at other times leaving it for him to open; and by abating or increasing his own pace, accommodate his precepts to the capacity of his pupil."—MONTAIGNE.

IT may at once be said that there must be a great desire, almost an anxiety to learn, on the part of the pupil. There must also be, in order that teaching may be thoroughly effectual, a true and deep sympathy between the pupil and the tutor. Experience shows that good guidance is required to advance greatly in any subject and certainly is it most necessary, if one wishes to learn as quickly, as easily, and as well as possible. In learning to play any musical instrument help is especially requisite. So many little practical details are met with, a knowledge of which can scarcely be gained without the aid of one who knows them. It is really impossible to learn from books, thoroughly, by one's self alone. Oral instruction and practical exemplification are indispensable for those who would excel in playing any instrument. In the case of the most difficult of all musical instruments, the violin, this is especially true. It is so easy to contract bad habits in playing, and so extremely difficult to abandon faults, that the advantages of learning under the supervision of a good teacher are manifestly apparent. Great loss of time is involved in unlearning what has been learnt wrongly. It is, moreover, essential to begin with a good master at once, and an effort must be made to find the best teacher procurable. The money expended on lessons is very well spent. It is not uncommon to suppose that the elements of violin playing can be learnt without help. Some wish to acquire at least the power of playing the different notes, and will insist on trying what they can do unaided for a few weeks or months. Their object is to master the rudiments, and thus to go equipped with a certain amount of knowledge to a tutor. Some even hope to test their ability before really commencing in earnest, fancying it best to settle beforehand, whether the difficulties will be so great as to deter them at the outset, and cause them to renounce the instrument altogether, or not. This is a great mistake. As a matter of fact, the beginner may be assured that by trying in this way much time will be lost. With regard to capacity, a good tutor will certainly be able to give a very definite opinion after a few lessons. Even if the ear or the power is condemned, the student has the satisfaction of having had a fair chance.

The little details essential in the correct tuning and holding of the instrument, in placing the fingers, using the bow, and so on, are so numerous, and must be attended to so exactly, that one cannot possibly gain a knowledge of them in the absence of practical instruction. No book, however clear, plain, and trustworthy it may be, can afford sufficient help.

In selecting a teacher, it is right to find out the best

INTRODUCTORY.

man, and one should not be too particular as to the price to be paid for the lessons. The learner will find that if trouble has been taken to secure the very best teacher practicable, much vexation will be saved. With regard to this matter, it is very possible to be penny-wise and pound-foolish, for there are some men who can teach more in an hour than others can in a month. The labourer is worthy of his hire. It is not, of course, to be supposed that the value of lessons is to be entirely judged by the price demanded for them; but it is not of the least use to hope to learn the fiddle well, unless one at least makes up one's mind to have a good tutor.

If you have made a wise selection, you will be able to rely entirely on your tutor, and this feeling alone will impart that confidence, which in itself is so valuable. It must be remembered that teaching the violin is very arduous work. The knowledge required necessitates not only a long course of training, but also great natural powers. We do not maintain that it is necessary to learn from a finishing master at the outset. Such a tutor, if asked for his advice, would probably recommend a thoroughly good man, by whom all the rudiments can be well taught. Although a good teacher will always be able to command a higher price than an inferior one, still it may sometimes happen that a really first-rate man may not be sufficiently well known to ask more than a moderate sum. If possible, the advice of some eminent or leading violinist should be sought before making arrangements. Above all, be sure you find a good violinist. There is in human nature a faculty of imitation, unconscious as well as conscious, which exerts a very considerable influence on our habits of thought and practice. You hear the instruction of your teacher, you observe his method of playing, you hear the tones emanating from his instrument, and unconsciously as well as consciously you learn to imitate him. Originality, the gift of the great, is not, of course, to be lightly esteemed; but every man must learn. This was so with Paganini, and has been the case with all our great players. The correctness and precision of tone, tune, and time, of the really good violinist will linger in the mind; and one naturally feels an incentive and a stimulus to play in the same manner and with the same or even greater perfection, were it possible. Moreover, lacking a standard with which to compare one's self, one is apt to grow careless, and perhaps to rest content with any sort of playing which is not quite execrable.

For this reason also, it is very desirable indeed that the beginner should take every opportunity of hearing and seeing the leading violinists.

The marvellous power and execution of a Joachim, Neruda, or Carrodus, playing the finest and deepest classical music with ease and precision, will stir one up to an enthusiasm, which will help to carry one through great labour. This is a point on which much stress should be laid, the more so since it applies universally. Many a man has been reclaimed from a life of idleness and carelessness by even a single interview with a leading personage. The untiring energy and unfailing industry of any active busy man constitute a standing rebuke to, and a keen and biting sarcasm upon, the paltry slipshod life. The power of the great is great indeed.

Lastly, it is to be remembered that a good tutor will continually repeat his instructions, and be extremely patient and enduring. It is not, however, always the case that the best players are the best teachers. Playing is an art in itself, and teaching is another art in itself. The two are quite distinct, and it may happen that an eminent violinist, even if he should happen to be a teacher, may scarcely possess the patience required for good and careful guidance.

A good tutor must know exactly how a thing should be done. More than this, he must know how to impart his ideas to his pupil. He must be able to tell exactly what to do, and possess the power of showing how to do it.

He should show the utmost sympathy with his pupils, and make it felt that he earnestly desires their progress.

INTRODUCTORY.

He should be on the watch for the slightest error of any kind.

The pupil should make not only a mental note, but also a written one, of all the faults which most seriously beset him. Pupils frequently, through fear of trying unduly the patience of the tutor, pretend they understand a thing when they do not. Especially do they do this, when signs of irritation are displayed. On no account whatever should they act thus. On the contrary, let the pupils ask as many questions as they like. They should take care to understand the exact meaning of the tutor's remarks. The time thus spent is far from being wasted.

Above all, it is necessary for the learners to concentrate the mind intensely on details, which may even seem to be at first unimportant.

It is these small differences in playing which make all the difference between good and bad violinists.

Again, however good teaching in class may be, and however useful in producing the capability of keeping good time, in imparting confidence to the player, and in many other ways; it must be understood that no beginner can dispense with private instruction.

The two kinds of teaching, viz., class teaching and private instruction, should go on together, helping and aiding each other.

Never should pupils be discouraged, while learning, by what any one may say. A good and clever teacher will never discourage his pupils. He will tell them of their faults, but will not expatiate upon them to such a degree as to dishearten: nor will he lose his temper if the learner seems stupid or slow. The best masters, too, will not omit to remark excellences as well as deficiencies. They give blame where blame is due, but they will also give praise where praise is due. It is utterly impossible for the pupils to know how they are playing unless comments of both kinds are uttered.

B. Instruction-Books.

" 'Tis but instruction, all ! "—Aaron Hill.

It is certainly best to begin with an elementary work. The exercises cannot be too simple at first. They should also be progressive in character, and the easy ones should lead up to the more difficult by gradual steps. The tutor whom you have chosen must be your guide in the selection of an instruction-book. He will be able to recommend the one most suitable for the particular method of teaching he is in the habit of pursuing, and it will be wise to follow his advice implicitly in this, as in all other matters connected with your study. It may be added that instruction-books almost invariably require to be supplemented by manuscript exercises, and that your tutor will not only be able to guide you best with regard to the particular book to be used, but will also be ready to supply all written additional exercises that may be needed in your case.

It is not advisable for the pupil to be fond of picking out tunes, nor should he or she be easily dissatisfied, if it appears that there are too many dry exercises to be practised.

Some beginners are apt to think that their progress in playing a musical instrument is to be tested by the number of tunes they can play. This is far from being the case, since it is a comparatively easy matter to play so as to satisfy the ear of an average listener, but a very different thing to be able to play accurately, and with good execution. Similarly, the parents of children who can play on the piano the "Blue Bells of Scotland," "Home! Sweet Home!" and a few operatic airs, often think the progress made is rapid and good, whereas it may, on the contrary, be very bad. Scales and exercises must be assiduously practised, if one wishes to become a really good player on any musical instrument. This remark is particularly and in the highest degree applicable in the case of the violin.

INTRODUCTORY.

Scales may be called the ladder of music, and it is only by mounting this ladder very carefully, that we can reach its highest rung. It is *possible* altogether to dispense with instruction-books, books of exercises, or even the scales, as simple tunes can be learnt off by heart and played by ear. Those who pursue this method generally omit a bar or so here and there, and play out of time, dwelling upon some favourite notes, in order to "draw out the expression." As a matter of fact, the power of playing an instrument by ear, *i.e.*, to be able to fish out unconsciously the notes of a tune, is no great accomplishment; and yet there are some who are very proud of their capacity for so doing. This elementary form of playing entirely by ear is a ruinous practice, and gives rise to the murdering of music. Learn a piece of music thoroughly, so as to remember it without the help of notes, if you like. Having done this, a written score is neither necessary nor desirable. In fact, we hold that if perfection is sought after, music should be, where practicable, learnt so exactly that it can be produced without mnemonical aid of any kind.

It may be well just to mention some instruction-books.* Davids', Spohr's, and a famous school by Rode, Balliot and Kreutzer, Loder's, Hermann's, and Berthold Tour, are all very good. Kreutzer's is *par excellence* the book for "studies." One can practice the exercises in his work over and over again, without being tired of them. The question of types depends in a great measure upon one's eyesight. Of foreign editions those of Peters and those of Litolff, are strongly to be recommended for the accuracy, clearness, and smallness of the type.

---

* For further information on this and on allied subjects, the reader will do well to apply, personally if possible, or by letter, to Messrs. Reeves, " Musical Directory," 185, Fleet Street, London, E.C., or to some other celebrated and highly esteemed firm.

C. Practice:

" Excellence is never granted to man but as the reward of labour
—Sir Joshua Reynolds,

A few words on this most important subject will not be out of place. It is essential to devote much time to practice; but make up your mind at once not to be discouraged by remarks you will probably frequently hear on this subject. It is quite true that in order to play the violin perfectly, or indeed to play any other instrument as well as it can be played, a lifetime's devotion to the subject is required; but it is not to be forgotten that there are many very good amateur musicians who have not been able to afford very much time. You may be told that if you practise twelve hours a day for twenty years or so, you will possibly be able to play the fiddle tolerably at the end of that period. Now, this is only another way of saying that the violin is a most difficult instrument, and that to please by fiddling, a higher degree of skill is required than would be necessary in the case of pianoforte-playing or singing. Amateurs, as a rule, cannot possibly give up so much time. The fact is, that in talking of difficulties, people are apt to be inaccurate. Some they magnify, some they lessen. The best plan is to give as much time to your study as you can spare, and to make the best of it. You should at least practise for two or three hours every weekday. The Sunday's rest will be found beneficial; since you will find *at first* that a little intermission now and again will do no harm, but rather good.

Many beginners say that the more they play the worse they seem to play. It appears to them that practice does not improve them. The reason of this is, that by constant practice, one becomes better able to distinguish time, tune, and tone, and thus one's playing strikes one as being worse than at first, although in all probability it is very much more more correct. There can be no

INTRODUCTORY.

doubt that a thorough appreciation of, and an ear for, the essentials of good music are acquired with comparative ease and rapidity; whereas the power to produce, by the medium of the fingers and hands on a difficult instrument, what the brain dictates, is a far more serious task, and consequently of much slower growth. When tired out, or when suffering from weakness or illness, one who knew well how a piece of music ought to be played, could scarcely carry out his ideas well in practice. At the same time, it must be remembered that the understanding and appreciation of good time, tune, and tone must be possessed, in order that the music may be suitably interpreted. It is manifest that those who, while being highly endowed in this respect, suffer from weakness of the fingers or hands, can never play with accuracy. On the other hand, people possessing the greatest flexibility and power of fingers and joints, and the utmost capability of using hands and fingers with dexterity, who at the same time have not the necessary mental qualifications, such as a good ear for time, tune, and tone, can do nothing on the violin.

It is, without doubt, advisable and wise to accustom one's self to different violins. Some persons omit to do this. The tutor will probably lend you different violins during the lesson, if he can trust you with them.

In playing, above all things avoid self-consciousness, Many players and singers spoil their efforts by their nervousness. Especially is it advisable to overcome such feelings. Many of the cleverest people are extremely nervous at first; but gradually gain confidence as they become accustomed to public or private performances.

It should be one's effort to become completely forgetful of self. This is at once extremely difficult and extremely important. People who are very self-conscious lose confidence, when others are listening to them, imagining themselves to be criticized. Hence they break down wholly or partially. Try to be so wrapt up in your playing that nothing can disturb you. One should seize every opportunity of practising one's playing before friends, and before strangers. Thus confidence will be gained, and that feeling of nervousness, which is so fatal to those who possess it, will be lost. Any public performance, whether public speaking, singing, acting, reciting, or playing any musical instrument, must be more or less spoiled by nervousness. Undue self-consciousness when playing the violin is especially apt to bring one to grief—more so, indeed, than in the case of any other performance. Unless the violin is carefully, confidently, and artistically played, not only may tones be produced which are harsh and squeaking, but also noises which are ludicrous in the extreme. The risible faculties of the audience may be aroused, and then there is for the time being an end to your confidence, if not your playing. It is, in fact, far better to stop than to go on from bad to worse; otherwise that may befall you which happened to the gentleman who was trying to sing "*Meet* me once again." He was interrupted by a violent and prolonged scratching on the outside of the door. It turned out to be the cat.

Remember, too, that in many people's estimation a great violinist is merely a good fiddler, while a bad or imperfect one is a legitimate subject for ridicule, if not for contempt, even should he be such an one as—

> "Ralph Rasper, who's an honest man,
> Prone to do all the good he can.
> He never lets the piteous poor
> Go meatless from his open door;
> He loves his wife; he pays his bills,
> And with content his household fills.
> He seeks, in short, the rule of right,
> And keeps his conscience pretty white.
> But save, oh, save us from his fiddling!
> It is so very, very middling!"
>
> (From George Dubourg).

Remember also, however, that "great works are performed not by strength, but by perseverance" (Johnson).

and that "a falling drop at last will cave a stone" (Milton.) The beginner may be sure that, with earnest perseverance, she or he will play better and better, as years roll on.

CHAPTER II.

REMARKS ON THE PURCHASE OF YOUR VIOLIN.

A. IMPORTANCE OF BUYING A GOOD VIOLIN.

ANY instrument, it is often said, will suffice for the purpose of learning the notes and the method of fingering. It is quite true that one may learn the notes on an inferior violin, *after a fashion.* This, however, is not what is wanted. It is necessary to learn well from the beginning, and we maintain that the use of a bad violin at first is exceedingly injudicious. [There are persons who, having pursued this method for the space of some months, have become wearied and disgusted with their fruitless efforts, and have ended by abandoning altogether their attempt to learn the fiddle. The same holds, in fact, with regard to all activities. People are fond of mentioning the cases of great artists, who have begun by drawing pictures with chalk and charcoal on the sides of humble tenements, or by fashioning the mud gathered from neighbouring gutters. It is true that great ends have often had small beginnings, but none the less true is it that in order to do things really well, certain conditions are absolutely essential. Of course, a man or woman of genius is not to be cramped up and kept out of sight by even serious obstacles. Rather will every difficulty be overcome, and every advancing foe disarmed. Still even the greatest are the better able to cope with stumbling-blocks, which are necessarily impeding the onward path of all, when those which are avoidable have been removed. There is present in each man or woman a certain amount of power or force, and that amount is capable of accomplishing a definite sum of work. Is it not, then, important to take care that all this energy is used in the right direction, and that it is not needlessly expended in overcoming obstacles which need not be encountered?

Violins vary greatly in tone, and it is of great importance that one should secure from the very first an instrument characterised by what is called a "good tone." The beginner will be obliged to exercises the greatest care in order to prevent "scratching and squeaking," and he certainly should not add to his difficulties by using a bad fiddle.

Even when tune and time are acutely observed by a player, an instrument of bad tone spoils all; for it is possible to play the fiddle, or to sing, in perfect tune and time, and yet to distress the ears of listeners by playing or singing without good tone. Nothing can be worse for the learner than to gain false ideas of notes, chords, and scales from efforts on a violin which, even in the hands of a practised player, could not be made to produce a good tone. [Great violinists may accomplish much with inferior instruments, no doubt; while not only may bad players be able to do very little with fine ones, but they may even spoil them to some extent by faulty manipulation.] It is, then, imperatively necessary that the pupil should not be handicapped by learning to play on an instrument with which it is impossible to produce what is so essential in music, viz., a good tone or quality of sound. A fairly good violin will serve one's purpose at first; but, as proficiency is gained, it will be well to purchase a fiddle of really fine tone. Let it be remembered that all the great violinists use, as is natural, the very best instruments which can be procured. When it is possible, they obtain one either by Antonio Stradivari, the greatest of all violin-makers; or by the great Joseph

Antonius Guarnerius, called Joseph del Jesu, from the circumstance of a cross and the letters "I. H. S." being found in almost all his tickets; or by Nicholas Amati, or by other old makers. These old violins are the best; but there are very good ones of recent manufacture. If the beginner can afford to expend a large sum, let him procure at the outset, *under the supervision of the tutor, or some thoroughly trustworthy connoisseur*, a violin of first-rate quality, and then musical taste and diligent and prolonged application, with good tuition, will supply all the essentials for future excellence.

B. How to set about securing a Good Violin.

Having, then, concluded that it is very necessary indeed to possess a good violin, let us now consider how best to procure one. It is quite possible to give thirty shillings, or even two or three guineas, or more, for an instrument that is not worth five shillings. Moreover, it is not unfrequently the case that the seller is not consciously cheating or misleading, when this happens; for it may be that, although he knows a great deal about other subjects, such as pianos and music, for example, still he has very little intimate acquaintance with the violins exposed for sale. The instruments may have been bought without due care, or possibly there may have been wanting in the buyer the qualities required in order to be able to test them properly. A dealer in violins may have been himself deceived by the recommendation of the person from whom he purchased them, or he may have bought them haphazard at a sale. Perchance he trusted to a certain exterior beauty.

It may happen too that the amateur violinist fancies that he can procure a good violin at a cheap price at a sale. He must, however, be very careful. If he wishes to attend an auction, let him on the view day take a competent judge with him, and have the actual worth of the violin stated. Many persons have bought inferior violins at sales, at fabulous prices. This comes partly from the excitement consequent on a sale, partly from an idea that the violin is really worth the price to which it has already run, and partly from the difficulty of getting a good sight of it. A friend of ours purchased a violin at a sale some time ago for three guineas. It was not worth fifteen shillings. The top of the scroll was carved out in the shape of a man's head. He vaguely conceived that this latter circumstance was a proof of its being an old one, forgetting that though it might be ancient, it might also be bad. Probably his excitement was observed by others and by the autioneer, and then the instrument was run up to the price of three guineas It should not be forgotten that very long and careful study and a varied experience are required to make any one a really good judge of violins, and that the beginner should therefore always ask the advice and help of a first-rate violinist. It is, in fact, very injudicious to rely on any but the best men. Our advice is that the amateur should go to a good shop, to the establishment of a man well known as a connoisseur of violins—to such men as Mr. Hill or Mr. Hart, of 38, New Bond Street, for instance.

It is not really necessary that the beginner should have a fiddle by one of the old masters. These have not only a very large value in virtue of their extremely fine tone, but also what may be called a "fancy value," inasmuch as they are regarded as objects of rarity by collectors. One must in consequence expect to pay a very large price for them, seeing that there are people who are always ready and eager to procure them, even for extravagant sums. Many an amateur buys a violin with the label of a great maker inside it, either in writing, or in print. He pays a heavy price, and thinks, perhaps, that he has obtained a genuine instrument. Labels, of course, prove nothing. The fiddle may be one by a great master, but in the majority of cases it is only a copy, and a very worthless copy often enough. More than this, it may very possibly be a perfectly wretched instrument, with an atrocious tone. The old makers did use labels; but a label, even if the date be in accordance with the time at which the master lived, is far from being a guarantee of this master's handiwork. Sometimes, too, the labels were not dated; for instance, authentic tickets of Gasparo da Salò, who worked in Brescia from 1560 to about 1618, are said to be never dated. (This maker was the founder of the Brescian school, and the first to construct violins in their present shape.) Forgery has been practised to an almost incredible extent, and those who buy violins may suffer, unless, indeed, they exercise the greatest discrimination, from this form of dishonesty. As a matter of fact, there has been a very large amount of forgery and deceit with regard to violins, and it is especially difficult to detect it, inasmuch as a great deal of it was done very long ago. In fact, soon after each great master became famous, other makers preyed upon his name and reputation. It is said that even some of the greatest masters used the names of others to some extent, before their own fame was established. Germany has been severely censured for the sending out of large numbers of common fiddles, labelled with, and libelling, the names of the old makers, and worth only about one sovereign each. Many fine fiddles have been split up into pieces, in order that their different parts might be patched up with portions of inferior instruments. In this way genuine old instruments have been destroyed for the purpose of deception. A scroll by Stradivari, when placed upon a fairly good-looking instrument, might easily deceive the unwary. Mr. Huggins says truly that violins differ from each other in as many ways and as greatly as possible; that the cheapest are those into which has been infused the individuality of some great maker, and that a fine violin by Stradivari or by Guarnerius is cheap at five hundred pounds. Even a thousand pounds is not excessive for an undoubtedly fine violin. When we buy a good violin, we pay, as the Rev. H. R. Haweis says, for conditions which have passed away, for the inspiration of a matchless workman, and for the genius of a bygone age.

C. The Merits of Old Violins. Age and Use.

"My friend, the golden age hath pass'd away;
Only the good have power to bring it back.
Shall I confess to thee my secret thought?
The golden age, wherewith the bard is wont
Our spirits to beguile, that lovely prime,
Existed in the past no more than now;
And did it e'er exist, believe me still,
As then it was, it now may be restored."
Goethe.

"Not with the skill of an hour, nor of a life, nor of a century, but with the help of numberless souls, a beautiful thing must be done."
—Ruskin.

The age of a violin is a point in itself worthy of some special consideration. Although age undoubtedly improves a good violin, and although their age is one of the reasons why the violins of the old masters are so much better in tone than modern instruments, still it must not be supposed that it is this alone in which the difference lies. Generally speaking an old violin possesses a better tone than a new one; but we must bear in mind that it is only a good instrument which improves with being kept. A bad fiddle, *i.e.*, one which has been improperly made, can never be a good one. It will be manifest, then, that it is perfectly useless to store up inferior violins with the hope that, in virtue of being kept for some years, they will greatly improve as the wood becomes seasoned. On the contrary, even if most carefully preserved and played upon regularly, they will never be appreciably better, but may even become worse than at first. A good violin, however, will improve with age and with use by an experienced player.

Although, then, age and judicious employment improve good fiddles, bad ones, however old they be, will always remain bad. It is said that an old violin of good make will not unfrequently give out a bad tone, when played upon for the first time, after a long period of disuse. Of course, it may probably be that the instrument has been damaged; but it seems that the being well played upon, in itself, has a beneficial effect. Again, the tone of a fiddle is inseparably connected both with the treatment to which it is subjected, and with the method of playing upon it, so that a hasty, bad, or ignorant player might easily make a mistake in pronouncing a good violin to be one of inferior quality. In connection, however, with the fact that a really good violin may at first, or after an interval of repose, sound badly, it seems well to quote from a writer of a treatise on the violin (J. A. Otto), who makes the following observations on this point:—

"When a new violin is first strung, the tone is clear, harmonious, and easily produced; but after exercising it for eight days, it becomes harsh and offensive to the ear, so that the instrument seems as if it would never be fit to be heard again. In this second stage, perhaps, the greatest number of instruments are spoiled from the want of patience in the possessor, by scraping out the wood, changing the bass bar, and other fancies. Those also which are too weak in the wood now become bad, and do not improve afterwards. They never reach the third stage; but, by persevering in the practice of two notes together (in the case of good violins), the third stage is gradually attained, at which the instrument, like wax, receives every impression, and the tone, having recovered its power and fulness, again becomes clear and beautiful. This takes three months to effect."

There can be no doubt that some have discarded good violins, and perhaps have sold them for a small price; because while in their hands they have passed into the second stage. This, however, does not arise so much from impatience, as from ignorance of the facts mentioned above.

A violinist buys a really good instrument, which has not been used for some time; he wipes off the dust, strings his fiddle with the best strings, and begins to play. To his astonishment he is distressed by the sounds issuing from it, and it is not until he has patiently cajoled the spirit of his fiddle day by day for a considerable period, that his efforts are rewarded with well-merited success. There is, moreover, a mode of explaining this seemingly strange and almost incredible fact. The following remarks of a great scientist of the present day (Tyndall) are very noteworthy in this connection :—"The sonorous quality of the wood of a violin is mellowed by age. The very act of playing also has a beneficial influence, apparently constraining the molecules of the wood, which in the first instance might be refractory, to conform at last to the requirements of the vibrating strings." Is it not possible that the second stage referred to by Otto, may be produced during the time when the molecules are rearranging themselves, *i.e.*, while the alteration in their position is taking place? The beneficial influence of use applies equally to new instruments, as well as to old ones which have been laid aside for some considerable time.

The question still remains, Why do the old violins, as a rule, sound better than those of more recent make? It is indisputable that the genius and talent of the old makers, their comprehension and love of the art of violin-making, enabled them to construct far better violins than any now made. May it be possible that in the future the best fiddles of to-day will improve so much as almost to equal those of Stradivari at the present time? Though it is greatly to be feared that a distinct negative must be the answer to this query, there is no doubt that the mellowness of tone of the old violins is partly due to the fact that the wood has become seasoned by being kept for years, carefully preserved from decay. It probably loses its moisture, and becomes less easily acted upon by such external influences as changes of temperature, and of degrees of moisture in the air. One of the difficulties involved in the manufacture of good violins is the complete preparation and preservation of the wood. It is said that the wood must be cut only in December and in

January, and that only that part which has been exposed to the sun must be used.

The violin-makers of Cremona and the other celebrated towns of Italy were probably far more careful than are their successors of to-day. Each little detail of the art was thoroughly attended to. The selection of the most suitable wood, and the preparation and preservation of it were considered to be of the very highest importance. The wood of which a violin is made must be completely and entirely dry. The process of drying must be accomplished naturally, and not artificially. It occupies as much as five or six years. Some makers have tried the artificial process of baking the wood. The tone is thus made good for a time, but does not last. Other methods also have been tried.

Strange as it may seem, we cannot now produce violin-varnish equal to that used by the old masters. They probably used the soft resins, such as mastic, sandarach, benzoin, and perhaps soft copal or dammar. The same style of varnish, with variations of colour and probably slight differences of preparation and material used, endured for nearly a hundred years. It was employed by nearly as many violin-makers in different places down to the time of Stradivari, when the preparation of varnish made a considerable advance. This so-called amber varnish was the ordinary varnish of commerce at that time. It was only discarded when the spirit varnishes, which are more suitable for general use, though not for violins, were first made. We are now unable to dissolve suitably the resins employed. It is also a matter of some considerable difficulty to select the best colouring matter, and to prepare it. It has recently been given out that the secret has been discovered; but our readers will recognise that, if so they will probably soon hear more about it. It is, moreover, almost impossible to subject the Cremonese varnish, in its present condition, to a satisfactory chemical investigation. Some of the constituents are oxidized, and possibly otherwise chemically altered. Again, there are not many possessors of genuine instruments who would allow the varnish to be analyzed. It could not be replaced. Those who have had much to do with old Italian instruments, and have tried to clean them, know how difficult it is to avoid taking off some of the varnish. Though these varnishes have been closely imitated, it is always possible to distinguish the genuine from the new. In the case of the old fiddles, the excellent varnish used has soaked thoroughly into every part of the sycamore and deal wood, so that now they are capable of resisting effectually almost every decaying influence.

In short, it may be said that, just as the old painters possessed powers which are not met with now, and just as the inspiration which prompted and produced the old cathedrals and churches is wanting in our time, so in the case of violins the odour of antiquity brings with it a special charm.

There are violin-makers of the present day—as possibly also poets, painters, and architects—who maintain that their productions nearly equal those of olden times. At the Inventions Exhibition of London, in the present year (1885), violins of superior make are displayed. These, according to some, approach in excellence those of the old Italian masters. It may be so. Let us, therefore, hope that in the not-distant future the art of making really fine instruments which has been lost, may be found again. Nay, more, let us hope that we have passed through one of those temporary retrograde waves, which necessarily mark all progress. Let us look for even better violins than any that have yet been produced. Nothing can be a more pleasing feature of this enterprising and progressive age, than the enthusiastic attempts now being made to emulate those excellences, which were due to the labours of love of our forefathers. Let us not refrain from aiming at those grand and great works of the past to which misleading timidity might forbid us to aspire.

We remark, with Mr. Higgins, that in violins, as in all things else, there has been a slow but sure evolution. How can we say that the highest and most perfect form has already been reached? "Is there no place left for another Stradivari?" The distinctive characters of the tone of a violin by Guarnerius as compared with that of one of

Stradivari's finest instruments, might suggest the possibility of some delicate modification of form which should combine the powerful and mellow richness of the one with the brilliancy and universal adaptiveness of the other.

Let us never forget, while striving after perfection, Milton's beautiful words—

> "Yet I argue not
> Against Heaven's hand or will, nor bate a jot
> Of heart or hope, but still bear up and steer
> Right Onward."

D. Testing or Making Trial of a Violin.

> "Trial alone of ill and folly gives
> Clear proofs of the world's vanities."
>   BAILEY.

Whoever has listened with enthusiasm to a fine singer or instrumentalist of genius, will recognise that there is something over and above good tune, time, and execution in really good performances. There is " fine tone." When one hears a piano in good preservation, by Erard, or Collard, or Broadwood, beautifully played, one appreciates at once what tone is. When one hears a fine violin by Stradivari, still more clearly is " good tone " to be noted.

Although, therefore, one must by trial alone find out clear proof of the world's vanities, by trial also will one be able to find and to acknowledge what is good.

Let us consider how a violin of good tone can be best tested. The trial of a piano is a much more easy matter than the testing of a tone of a violin. The tone and quality of a piano may be fairly well judged of in a few moments.

To estimate the value of a violin great care and atten

tion are needed. Even a good fiddle may not sound well at first, and there are many diverse conditions to be considered. The place, the atmosphere, the skill on the part of the player, the kind of strings used, the temperature, degree of moisture, and other external influences, are all apt to vary so much, as to make a decision exceedingly difficult.

For instance, with faulty or bad strings a good instrument would, of course, sound badly. Again, with regard to a piano, the maker's name is, generally speaking, a sufficient guarantee, although forgery is possible even in the case of pianos. It is, however, quite enough in the general way to see, for instance, the name Erard, or Collard, or Broadwood, on a piano. Of course, their pianos may be worn out, or out of tune, or deranged, or badly preserved. We remember once hearing of an instance of forgery which is said to have been perpetrated in some part of South America. The name of some famous piano-maker was given to a large number of worthless instruments, and we are told that the consequence is that even to this day real pianos by this celebrated maker are there regarded with suspicion. Be this as it may, there is no doubt that modern pianos are the best, while, on the contrary, the violins of the old masters are of matchless excellence; and when we add to this the fact that extensive forgery has been going on ever since the time when they were made, it will be evident that the beginner must not rely on his or her judgment as to the genuineness or excellence of a fiddle.

An experienced player, as a rule, however, will know how to test a violin, and the learner will, therefore, do well to seek the counsel of such an one.

For the benefit, however, of those who wish or are compelled to test instruments without the aid of a good violinist, a few words of caution will not be misplaced. In case you should desire to buy a violin, if possible, hire it for a week or so. Take it to a small room in your house, place on it a best set of strings, tune it to the proper pitch, and play upon it single and double stops.

The more crowded with curtains, furniture, and hangings, the room may be, the better.

You and your friends should judge if the tone be pleasing or harsh. A musical ear will be pained by a harsh, nasal, or woody tone. If you are not a good fiddler you must make arrangements for having the instrument played properly by some one else: since a good instrument will not sound well, unless it is played by one who knows how to play.

It would be well to remark here, that a bad violin will not bear much pressure. Its badness will be more particularly discernible if it is played upon powerfully. A good violin will bear any reasonable amount of pressure on the strings; but a bad one cannot bear this test.

It must not be forgotten that a poor violin sounds fairly well in the open air, or in a large empty room, or on the landing of a large and high staircase, where plenty of resonance is imparted.

A friend of ours, who wished to buy a violin once fell into error, owing to forgetfulness of this point. He tried a fiddle on the large stone staircase of a large building. The instrument sounded well; but, on taking it to his own home, the apparent difference in tone was marked and unmistakeable. Of course there was no real difference except in the surroundings.

Always test your violin in a small room, or in a large room well filled with furniture and hangings, where poverty of tone is distinctly discernible. It is well to bear in mind, too, that the notes produced by an instrument of good timbre are carried to greater distances than those emitted from fiddles of bad tone.

If the hearers are situated in the lower rooms of a house while the player performs in an attic, they will be the better able to pronounce a correct judgment with regard to tone. There is a peculiar penetrating power noticeable in the sound of a good violin, so that the softest *pianissimo* notes can be heard distinctly and clearly at a great distance. On the occasion of a visit, about a year ago, to a small hall in Piccadilly although seated only a short distance from a solo violinist, I and others near me were greatly struck by the fact that his *pianissimo* notes were quite inaudible. This was no doubt due to defectiveness of the instrument used.

Rather different is the following more or less authentic case. A violinist, hearing a street-fiddler, was not only astonished at the beautiful mellowness of the sound, but also surprised by its peculiarly penetrating quality. He took steps, with the man's permission, to have the violin judged by a connoisseur, and it was found to be, strange to say, a genuine instrument by one of the old masters. Eager amateurs! ever be on your guard!

In relation to this part of our subject, we would call the attention of the reader to a popular fallacy, viz., the idea that noise and power are the same thing, and that a violin cannot at the same time possess both mellowness and power. This is an erroneous belief. The word *loud* has attained, by conventional use, the significance of "noisy." As a matter of fact, it is just this "noisy" intonation that is lost in a large building full of persons. In the case of violins being played together, other things being equal, it is the one which is most powerfully played upon that is heard above the rest. Where, however, the other things are not equal, that is, when the tones of the instruments vary greatly, the one which has the purest tone, even though played moderately loud, will be distinct from the other ones with bad tone, even if these are played *forte*. The softest *pianissimo* notes of a fine violin may be heard all over a large concert-hall, while those of an inferior instrument, though played with equal skill would not penetrate very far.

At the Albert Hall, when Strauss himself plays along with his orchestra, as he does from time to time, as a matter of fact the notes of his violin are to be distinguished from the rest. The same remark applies to the human voice, and hence it is that the *pianissimo* notes of a great solo-singer can be heard in every part of a large opera-house. It is, however, possible that a violin might be heard individually on account of its bad qualities, or of faults in the playing. The acoustic properties of the building have much to do with the propagation and conduction of sound-waves.* Similarly with regard to public speaking, an orator or preacher who possesses the requisite qualities of voice can without effort make himself heard distinctly throughout a densely packed assembly. It is not so much that an irregular, harsh, and noisy tone is quite lost, as that it falls on the ear without any definiteness or clearness. If we remember that a musical sound is produced by pulses or waves of motion, which follow each other at regular intervals, and that noises are the result of an irregular succession of waves, we shall be prepared to understand how it is that we hear musical sounds more readily than noises. The brain, by the medium of the ears and auditory nerves, receives in the one case similar stimuli at equal intervals of time, and is therefore more ready to recognise them. In the case of noises, the sound-waves are so irregular, that the brain is confused and disturbed. In order to acquire the power of testing a violin properly, it is necessary to have a knowledge of, and a taste for "good tone." It is recorded of Mozart that when he was a boy he called a violin with a full, soft tone a "butter-violin." This term is a very expressive one, as it stands out in direct opposition to all that is harsh and grating. The word "mellow" is conventionally used to express this perfection of tone.

Before concluding this chapter, it seems well to repeat that it is a matter of extreme difficulty to determine the quality of a violin, and therefore to procure a good one.

---

* We should like to see the experiment tried of having a building constructed so as to be perfectly and uniformly spherical in shape. It would, doubtless, be inconvenient to have a deeply curved floor; but it might be managed by a skilful architect. Then we would have the violinist perched in the very centre of the sphere, in order that the waves of sound might be propagated with absolute symmetry to all parts, and that the reflected waves of sound might also be unerringly equal.

Firstly, it is exceedingly important that the beginner should secure a good fiddle.

Secondly, in order to do so, the best advice must be sought.

Thirdly, special knowledge is required in order to be able to know a violin by one of the old masters; and these old fiddles are undoubtedly the best.

Fourthly, the instrument should certainly be tested by playing.

Finally, let it be added that even when fiddles do not give out a bad tone, they are often nevertheless very defective. They may give out a nasal or a woody tone, and this may either be due to a permanent defect in the general make of the instrument, in which case a connoisseur would know, or the fiddle may be out of condition, and require careful repairing by a good violin-doctor, as will be seen in the next chapter.

We would add that a violin should be, if possible, equally good in all its parts, that is to say, granting that the player has stringed his instrument with good strings, the *tone* of *each* string should be good. There are many *fiddles* which are only good in regard to one or two strings.

CHAPTER III.

THE PRESERVATION AND REPAIR OF FIDDLES.

LET us suppose that a good instrument has been obtained. Naturally it is very desirable to preserve it as well and as carefully as possible, so that its tone may be improved, and not deteriorated. Let us see how this can best be done.

A strong well-made wooden case, lined on the inside with baize, or still better with plush or velvet, is in many respects to be preferred to a leathern case. It is more securely air-tight, and is more protective, both directly,

THE PRESERVATION AND REPAIR OF FIDDLES

since it offers more resistance to pressure, and indirectly, in so far as an instrument kept in a wooden case is less liable to be subjected to changes of temperature, and to varying degrees of moisture in the atmosphere. If, however, a leathern case is used, it is best to have it lined on the inside with wadding or felt. The violin itself should always be enclosed in a baize bag opening at the wide end, though this is perhaps unnecessary, provided that it is kept in a well-lined case.

The box should have the name and address of the owner on the outside. When one has finished playing, it is necessary to wipe off the belly any resinous particles which may have dropped upon it from the bow. At the same time we would add a caution. Wipe the belly with a piece of clean silk, but on no account use a knife or sharp instrument for the purpose: otherwise you may scrape off some of the varnish, and thus render your violin liable to be affected by the moisture of the atmosphere and other agencies. It is also of the utmost importance to keep the instrument thoroughly clean. We cannot insist too strongly upon this point. Dirt tends to clog up the pores of the wood, and to spoil the tone-power of the violin.

When a violin is not being used, it is of paramount importance to place it where it will be perfectly safe. It is not impossible, if you are careless about this, to have your violin seriously damaged. This word of caution is not needless. Some difficulty may probably be experienced in finding, among the many ornamental but useless pieces of furniture in some drawing-rooms, a safe position for your poor violin. Do not put it on the floor. The lady of the house ought to provide for such matters, but she may, of course, be forgetful. It is to be hoped, now that ladies are beginning to play fiddles, that the fair sex will recognise the value of good ones. It is certainly to be presumed that the husbands of fair violinists will do so.

We are reminded here of a professional violinist who was unfortunate enough to leave his fiddle safely packed up, as he thought, in its leathern case in a railway carriage. For the sake of greater security, he had taken the precaution on getting out for the purpose of drinking a cup of tea, to lock the carriage door. A very stout lady, however, who happened also to possess a railway key, entered the carriage, thinking to be alone, and, as bad luck would have it, promptly sat down upon the case. What was our friend's horror, when he returned, to find the belly, bridge, and sound-post of his fine violin broken and shattered! He purchased a wooden case, after this mishap.

It is important to keep your fiddle as clean as possible, and not to let pieces of wood or string, or any stray particles, drop through the sound-holes. Occasionally it is well to clean the violin by pouring into it hot barley and shaking well. The dust which has accumulated is taken up by the barley, which must then be shaken out. Only very seldom indeed need this be done. It is an easier process than might at first sight appear, but requires some knack. Care should be taken not to allow the strings to become coated with dirt. In order to prevent the soiling of the strings, always have the fingers as dry and as clean as possible, before beginning to play. A piece of perfectly clean silk spread upon the top of the strings, while the fiddle lies in its case, may serve as a further protection for them.

Alway see that the neck of your violin is smooth, and free from dirt or grease; since otherwise the shifts cannot be manipulated with ease and dexterity.

Let the beginner be very cautious with regard to the repairing of his instrument, when it is out of order, or broken in any part.

He must take his instrument to the right man; and we would recommend Mr. Hill, of 38, New Bond Street, London, who has a reputation for knowing what ought to be done and how to do it. There are, on the other hand, so many botchers about, who, on the pretence of knowing how to mend violins, simply spoil them. It is mentioned by Otto that a certain person called Kirschlag, in 1787, made a visit of destruction, under pretence of repair, to most of the towns in Germany. Do not trust your violin indiscriminately into the hands of any one; but, in case of need, let a good and well-known repairer of violins correct the disorder or damage.

It is said that on one occasion, in the olden times, when stringed instruments were played in churches, a bill was sent to the vicar, worded as follows:—" 2s. 6d. to fettling a base villon "—and that the vicar wished all base villains could be fettled at the same easy rate.

CHAPTER IV.

A FEW SHORT REMARKS OF A GENERAL CHARACTER ON THE FIDDLE, TOGETHER WITH A BRIEF HISTORY OF SOME OLD MAKERS.

"Nothing good bursts forth all at once. The lightning may dart out of a black cloud; but the day sends his bright heralds before him, to prepare the world for his coming."—HARE.

A. GENERAL REMARKS.

WHEN we consider the many extreme difficulties which men encountered in their attempts to manufacture perfect musical instruments, we must feel the greatest astonishment at the degree of success achieved. It was only by the prolonged and persevering energy and industry of many, that we have been enabled to advance so far. How thankful ought we to be that we live in an age when so much of the hard rough work has been so well done! How glad we ought to feel that so many of the difficulties before us have been so far lessened; that now we can " make music sweetly blend with the grand harmony of the spheres "! There are, remarks a great writer, three classes of men—the retrograde, the stationary, and the progressive. Let us try, above all things, to belong to the last of these, and, while striving to advance, let us strive so strenuously as to ensure success.

We must the more admn_ the genius of the old masters, when we reflect upon the special difficulties involved in the manufacture of a perfect violin, and when we realise that each separate part and each characteristic, as well as the general form of the instrument, demanded the most steadfast attention, and the most indefatigable devotion to work. The history of violins furnishes us with a dim idea of the unremitting industry which was necessary to supplement and bring forth in perfection the genius of an Amati, a Stradivari, a Guarneri. It is easy to see that the final conformation of the fiddle is in accordance with acoustic principles, though those who determined it had but little knowledge how they were unconsciously finding the practical results and applications of scientific principles.

The capacity of the violin-box is practically the same in all the best fiddles; but there should be a due relation between the size of the resonance-box on the one hand, and the thickness of the wood on the other. If the volume of air capable of being contained is too large, notes of low pitch are rendered dull and weak, while the high notes possess a piercing quality. If, on the other hand, the capacity is too small, the deep notes are harsh and the first string lacks brilliancy.

Again, if the belly be either too thin or too thick, the resonance will be greatly impaired. The shape of the ƒ-holes and of the bridge, and the character of the incisions in the latter, are of great importance. It is said that Stradivari made an extensive series of experiments before finally deciding upon the patterns. The most important curves of the fiddle are those extending from side to side, and from top to bottom on the belly and the back. The musical instruments which preceded true fiddles were made flat like guitars. Afterwards different curves were tried. At length the exquisitely elaborated wavy lines of Stradivari were evolved. The greatest exactness is requisite in regard to the curves. For instance, if the arching of the belly is either too great or too small, the sounds emitted by the fiddle will be "nasal" or "muffled." The violin, though light and apparently fragile, is skilfully constructed and strong. Although it is impossible to exercise too much care in preserving a fiddle from damage, we should bear in mind that a good violin repairer can take it to pieces, and put it together again without injury. One would, however, hesitate to have this operation performed in the case of a fine old violin, unless it should be absolutely necessary.

In order that a fiddle shall be made, so as to be as perfect as possible, the most exact precision and accuracy in the manufacture and preparation of every part of it is, as we have said, indispensable. Not only must the instrument be perfect in form, but the wood must be most carefully prepared, and possess great elasticity. The various kinds of wood used must necessarily be of the correct thickness, of the right density, perfectly dry, and most artistically put together.

A fiddle consists essentially of two arched plates of wood, united by side-pieces to form a shallow box of an exact and definite shape and size. This cavity is constructed with a view to its powers of imparting resonance to differently pitched sounds. In the upper plate, which is sometimes called the belly, are two curved holes, shaped somewhat like an *f*, and termed the *f*, or sound-holes. This upper plate is of an arched form, with the convexity upwards. It is made of a soft elastic wood such as Swiss pine wood or deal. The lower plate, or back, on the contrary, must be of hard sonorous wood, such as sycamore or maple. The belly is supported by the sound-post, which is situated a little behind the right foot of the bridge. This is a little cylindrical pinewood prop, which conducts the vibrations, and also affects the nodal arrangement of the back and of the belly, by reason of its close contact with them. It is to be remarked that the quick and sharp vibrations of the hard wood blend with slower ones of the soft belly, in part through the medium of the sound-post in part through the volume of air contained in the violin-box. The two kinds of sound-waves, blending, give rise to the sweet, full, mellow, notes of a good violin. If all the wood were hard, the tone would be metallic and thin; if too thin, it would be flute-like.

At the sides, the upper and lower plates are united by means of six sycamore ribs, or side-pieces, bent so as to be of the correct form by the use of a heated iron, and supported by twelve blocks with linings, which secure the back and belly to the sides, and are made of pine or of lime-tree wood.

The pegs of a fiddle should be of box-wood, or better of rose-wood. The bass or sound-bar and the sound-post are made of pine-wood.

B. . A SHORT HISTORY OF SOME VIOLIN-MAKERS (FOR WHICH THE AUTHORS ARE INDEBTED MAINLY TO MR. JAMES W. FLEMING'S ABLE WORK, ENTITLED "OLD VIOLINS").

"We are such stuff
As dreams are made of, and our little life
Is rounded with a sleep."

There appears to be some slight evidence drawn from pictures in Etruscan and Greek vases belonging to the Prince of Canino, that instruments provided with the bow and bridge were known to the Greeks and Romans.

Hair for the bow, was, however, in all probability not used. Indeed, Paganini is reported to have played beautifully on his violin with a slender rush in a trial of skill between himself and a vain young man in Italy. If this be so, it is easy to understand that hair for the bow is not quite indispensable.

Whether it be true or not that the Greeks and Romans used such instruments, at any rate it seems certain that, as in the case of literature, painting, sculpture, and other branches of art, so in the case of violin-making, Italy may be said to be the birthplace of genius.

GENERAL AND HISTORICAL.

Passing over many names known as connected with violin-making, and merely mentioning the fact that about 1503 a picture was painted by Raphael, containing a viola with sound holes in the form of an *f*, while those formerly used were generally of the shape of two C's, placed face to face or back to back, we come to a short consideration of the Brescian school. From about 1560 to about 1610 Gasparo da Salò worked in Brescia. He is entitled to the credit of being the founder of the Brescian school, and also to that of being the first to construct violins in their present shape. The instruments of this maker are large and medium-sized. They are strongly arched. The soundholes are large. Their colour is dark brown or deep yellow, sometimes almost black. This is possibly owing to age. The wood used for the belly is very regular in the grain. The purfling is high, and the margins are large. It is probable that there are only three violins of this maker extant; but it is not certain where they are, or if they have been destroyed. There are, however, a number of violas, violoncellos, and double basses known. Authentic tickets of this maker are said to be never dated.

Other makers worked about this time; but the productions of this period of the Brescian school are characterised by fraud, fabrication, and duplicity. Instruments have been broken up and re-made, and tickets changed or imitated.

From about 1590 to 1640 Giovanni Paolo Maggini made splendid violins. He is the most eminent representative of the Brescian school. He is supposed to have been a pupil of Gasparo da Salò. His instruments are generally large; but some are medium-sized, and a few small. They are strongly arched, the curvature extending nearly to the purfling, which is generally double—a characteristic of the Brescian school. The rims or sides are somewhat low. The varnish is of a clear yellowish-brown colour, or golden yellow. The sound-holes are large and wide. Some of his tickets are not dated. Thousands of imitations have been made. The tone of his violins is grand and grave. The backs of some of his instruments are ornamented.

From about 1630 to about 1680 Pietro Santo Maggini worked in Brescia. His basses are very good, but his violins are not now known.

Let us consider very shortly the Cremonese school and its Italian followers. The founder of this school was Andreas Amati, who worked from about 1520 to 1580. His violins are of small and medium size. They are very strongly arched towards the middle. The varnish he used is somewhat thick, and of a clear brown or brownish-yellow, and sometimes transparent. The sound-holes are somewhat like those of Maggini. Probably very few of his instruments are left.

The sons of Andreas, viz., Antonius Amati and Hieronymus Amati, who flourished from about 1550 to about 1638, made very good fiddles, possessing a sweet and clear, but not very strong, tone. The wood for the breast is very close in the grain. They are almost always small, and the back is often in one piece. The varnish is very like that of Maggini, while the sound-holes are not unlike the earlier ones of Stradivari. The arching is raised towards the centre of the instruments.

Nicolas Amati, the greatest of this name, was the son of Hieronymus. He was born in 1596, and died in 1684. In his violins there is a greater delicacy of detail, and a greater perfection in the design of the curves. He flattened the model, extended the arching of both back and breast considerably towards the rims, and employed a brilliant varnish (golden red). The model is generally large, and the sound-holes are beautifully designed, though a little slighter than those of Stradivari. A fair number of his violins are still extant, and are worth upwards of £300 each.

Hieronymus, son of Nicholas, was the last Amati in Cremona. His violins are inferior.

The scooping at the sides and the high curves of the back and belly of the earlier violins by the Amati family prevent a grand tone. The tone, however, is sweet and full.

Now, passing over several names, we come to that of

Andreas Guarnerius, the first of this celebrated family. He was born in Cremona about 1625, was a pupil of Nicholas Amati, and probably worked from about 1650 to 1696. His work takes rank in the second order.

Joseph Guarnerius (Joseph, son of Andrew) is supposed to have worked in Cremona from 1690 to about 1730. His violins are much more highly valued than are those of his father, and almost all the best of them had tickets of his great relative, Joseph Antonius Guarnerius, placed inside, after the fame of the latter had spread. The pattern is small, and bears a striking general resemblance to that of Nicolas Amati. The *f*-holes have in the lower turn a long sweep, similar to those of his father. The varnish is of a brilliant red colour.

Pietro Guarnerius, second son of Andrew, worked at Cremona and at Mantua from about 1690 to 1725. His instruments are not highly esteemed.

A second Peter Guarnerius, son of Joseph Guarnerius, and grandson of Andrew, worked at Cremona and Venice from about 1730 to 1755. His work is praised, but lacks completeness.

The great Joseph Antonius Guarnerius, called "del Jesu,' from the cross and the letters "I.H.S." being found in almost all his tickets, was born in Cremona in 1683. He was the son of John Baptist Guarneri, who was a son of Andrew Guarnerius, but not a violin-maker, so far as is known His relationship to Andrew has been gleaned from the fact that some of the great artist's tickets contain the words "Andreæ nepos." Like those belonging to the early period of Stradivari, the early works of Joseph Antonius Guarnerius display but little originality, being, in fact, reproductions of the form and style handed down by Nicolas Amati to ancestors of the Guarneri family. During his second and third epochs, when he made his most excellent instruments he followed the best style of Stradivari. M. Fetis says that the violins of the second period are of small pattern, and happily designed. The arching is slightly elevated and falls off towards the purfling in a softly peaceful curve.

The violins of his third epoch are larger, made of splendid wood, and arranged beautifully with regard to the arching and the thickness of different parts. The varnish is very fine, and the instruments generally are quite equal to the best of Stradivari.

The last epoch, like that of Stradivari, is characterised by a marked diminution of power.

One of the finest and most renowned instruments by Joseph del Jesu is that which Paganini called his "canon." This was bequeathed to Genoa, where it lies silent and useless. It was the violin which Paganini took to Vuillaume, in Paris, for the purpose of repair. When the latter said that it must be opened, the great Genoese player insisted on the operation being done in his own presence, and at his own house. Next day the French maker called, and Paganini began to watch the operation with great nervousness. On the first "crack" being heard, the violinist started as if he had been stabbed, and, as the work went on, he seemed to suffer great agony. It was, after all, found necessary to let the fiddle remain with Vuillaume for some time, so that he had ample time to make an exact copy. He brought back the fiddle duly repaired, and afterwards showed Paganini his copy. The violinist tried it, and Vuillaume ultimately sold it to him for five hundred francs. It was left by Paganini to his pupil Sivori, who played on it ever after.

The great violins of Joseph Antonius Guarnerius are very graceful, and some are scarcely to be distinguished from those of Stradivari. The f-holes are, however, sensibly longer. There is great power in the design and execution of the scrolls. The name on the ticket of this master is, like so many others, Latinized. It is, in Italian, Guiseppe Antonio Guarneri. The letters "I.H.S." are accepted as the initials of "Jesus Hominum Salvator."

Antonio Stradivari, the greatest violin-maker who ever lived, is supposed to have been born in Cremona, in 1644, and to have died in 1737. His first works are said to bear the name of Nicolas Amati, whose pupil he was, but in 1670 he began to append his own name. From 1670 to

1690 he made very few instruments, and is supposed to have employed himself principally in making experiments and researches. He was in very comfortable circumstances, if not wealthy. About 1698 the character of his work diverged from that of Amati, and in 1700, when he was fifty-six years old, he attained that perfection which distinguishes his finest instruments during the next twenty-five years of his life. He seems to have devoted the whole of his long life to the steady pursuit of his profession. He is said to have been tall and thin, and to have worn a white leathern apron when working, a white wollen cap in winter, and a cotton one in summer.

Violins by Antonio Stradivari and the other great masters are extremely rare. For every hundred specimens supposed to be by Stradivari, it would be safe to reject ninety-nine as spurious. He may have made as many as six to seven hundred fiddles at the very most; and these, originally bought at a price ranging up to £3 10s., had been "knocked about" all over Italy and elsewhere for about one hundred and fifty years, before their merits attracted much attention. It was not until the beginning of this century that the great search for his instruments began. The great hunt is over, and the best fiddles all secured. The total number of genuine Stradivari violins now known in the various countries of Europe and in America does not, it is presumed, exceed two hundred.

The early violins of Stradivari are very like those of Nicolo Amati, under whose roof Stradivari worked; but they are of a higher order. Those produced between 1700 and 1725 are spoken of as belonging to "the grand period," or as being of "the grand pattern." His fiddles differ in form and in the colour of the varnish, which is always very fine. These instruments are characterized by a gradual and graceful arching, which extends almost to the purfling. In fact, the perfection of the curves contributes greatly to the fine quality of tone. The scientific precision of the form of Stradivari's fiddles has been acknowledged as quite unique. The scrolls are most artistic and beautiful, and their curves, though changing at every point, are yet marvellously combined. The greatest height of the centre of a fiddle by Stradivari, above the level of the rims, is about half an inch, while that of a fiddle of the Amati school is about one inch. The *f*-holes of the fiddles of this master are very beautiful, and may be said to be by far the best. All his best violins give one an idea of firmness, accuracy, and precision, combined with great delicacy and tenderness.

In the latest fiddles there is a falling off in the workmanship, as if the master were unable to carry out the practical details of his work, as in former days. It is said, however, that after his death some unfinished instruments in his workshop were sent out by his successors, with his name affixed to them. This dishonesty, coupled with more flagrant forms of fraud, may account for much of the alleged imperfection of his later work.

Joseph Antonius Guarnerius, mentioned above, is the only violin-maker who can be compared with Antonius Stradivarius. It was evidently the aim of the former great master to produce the deep, powerful, and richly mellow tone by which his fiddles are distinguished.

The two sons of Antonius Stradivarius who followed their father's profession were Francesco and Omobono. They both worked with their father until his death, and during that period their tickets bear the inscription—" sub disciplina Antonii Stradivari." Francesco seems to have made good violins from 1725 to 1742, bearing his own name; and Omobono chiefly occupied himself with repairing, but also made violins until 1742. Their instruments are mixed up with those ascribed to their father's last period.

Of the Italian pupils and imitators of Antonio Stradivari, Alessandro Gagliano is said to have been the son of a marquis, and to have been obliged to leave Naples on account of a murderous attack upon a man, who was about to marry a lady, to whom Gagliano was engaged. He concealed himself in a thick forest, and there amused himself by fabricating out of the trunks of trees, which he found at hand, instruments somewhat resembling the

GENERAL AND HISTORICAL.

violin. After some years, he returned to Naples, and founded there a violin-making business, which was continued through one or two generations. This clever and careful workman made some very fine instruments, and founded a distinguished family of fiddle-makers. He established himself in Naples about 1695. He left a son, called Gennaro Gagliano, who worked at Naples from about 1720 to 1750. There is said to be a violoncello in Paris made by him. Its excellence would certainly place the man who really made it in the front rank of makers.

There was a Nicolas Gagliano at Naples in 1777. Ferdinand Gagliano, a son of this Nicolas, lived at Naples at the end of the eighteenth century. These two last of the Gagliano family made comparatively poor instruments.

Carlo Bergonzi, the best pupil trained by Stradivari, worked in Cremona from about 1720 to about 1747. He may be said to complete the quartet of celebrated Cremonese makers. Nicolas Amati, Antonio Stradivari, Joseph Guarnerius, and Carlo Bergonzi lived in one generation. The first died in 1684, and the last about sixty years afterwards. There are only about fifty genuine instruments by Carlo Bergonzi. There are more violoncellos than violins by this maker. His varnish is reddish brown in colour, and sometimes seems to have been laid on too thickly, and to have cracked. His wood is generally fine. M. A. Bergonzi, son of Carlo Bergonzi, worked in Cremona until about 1758. His instruments are poor, as are also those of his two sons.

In the Cremonese and other tickets, the Latin name of the town terminates in various ways. One of these is "Cremone," which means "of Cremona."

"Cremonæ" is another form, which means "of Cremona," or "at Cremona."

"Cremona" signifies "in Cremona."

"Cremonensis" means "Cremonese," *i.e.* of or belonging to Cremona.

"Cremonen" is probably a contraction of "Cremonensis."

Old English fiddles are most serviceable. They possess a sweet and sometimes a really fine tone, and should be preferred to many second-rate and third-rate Italian instruments.

CHAPTER V.

DIFFERENT PARTS AND ADJUNCTS OF A VIOLIN.

A. THE SOUND-BAR AND SOUND-POST.

The Sound-bar.—The left foot of the bridge is to some extent supported by the sound-bar, just as, indeed, its right foot is by the sound-post. The sound-bar, or, as it is sometimes called, the bass-bar, is a strip of pine-wood, placed immediately under the left foot of the bridge. It has a sloping oblique position, and is stretched along the whole length of the left side, in a direction parallel to that of the strings, in order to facilitate the vibrations of the belly. At the present day it is longer and deeper near the centre, so as to support more perfectly the greater pressure resulting from the higher pitch now in vogue. Formerly it was not only shorter and slighter, but also inserted in a perfectly straight position. Experience has, however, led to the conclusion that there was thus produced a tendency to mute the instrument to some extent. By means of this girder the belly is strengthened at that part where the pressure is greatest, so as to render it capable of resisting the enormous force of the four strings. The pressure exerted in this way is said to be, in the case of a violin tuned up to a concert pitch, as much as that of a weight of ninety pounds. The utmost care is requisite in order to adjust correctly this support in each instrument, since a slight error in its position, a looseness or a roughness of finish, will give rise, when the fiddle is played, to that "hollow, teeth-on-edge-growl, called the 'wolf'" (Haweis).

The bass-bar is said to strengthen the tone in other ways, and not merely by reason of the support it affords to the belly and bridge.

The Sound-post.—The sound-post is a small cylindrical prop of about the diameter of a lead-pencil, which must be made of pine-wood and not of any other material. It is placed in an upright position inside the violin-box, and is fixed so as to support the belly. Its two extremities must be in close contact with the inner surfaces of the back and of the belly, and it should be situated so as to be from about $\frac{1}{8}$ to about $\frac{1}{4}$ inch behind the right foot of the bridge. If it were placed exactly under this foot of the bridge, the tone would be greatly impaired; but when it is a little behind the foot, a portion of the energy of vibration is directly imparted to the belly, and not conducted immediately to the back.

By the medium of the sound-post the short and long sound-waves unite and mingle. Very small differences in its position greatly modify the tone, and, as days may be spent in fixing it properly, it is advisable to take it at once, in case adjustment should be needed, to a thoroughly good violin-establishment.

As a general rule, in high-built violins and in weak ones it should be nearer the bridge than in the flatter fiddles. On the other hand, the low-built violins, in which the vibrations are more readily conducted from belly to back, require the sound-post to be further away from the bridge, so that the mingling of the sound-waves shall not be too rapid.

B. The Bridge.

The bridge must be neither too high nor too low, but exactly of the correct height, and of the right size and breadth. Each violin requires a bridge of special height. If the bridge is too high and too thick, and if, as a consequence of the undue height the strings are situated too far from the finger board, the sounds produced will be thin and dull, and brought out with difficulty. If, on the other hand, the bridge be too low, the tone will be shrill and powerless. By prolonged and careful observation one may be enabled to ascertain the correct height; but it will save a great deal of trouble to take an instrument to a good violin-maker, and have several bridges cut in accordance with its requirements. Four grooves must be made with care on the top of the bridge for the support of the strings. These must not be too deep, but just deep enough to prevent the strings from slipping off, and to keep them in fixed and definite positions, which should be equidistant from one another. The grooves should be semicircular and not angular, so that, being round in contour, the strings will rest nicely and evenly upon them without being cut. It is highly essential that there should be no intervening space between the strings and the grooves. Imperfect contact would give rise to the production of a bad tone. The bridge should be made of spotted maple-wood of medium density, and the grain of the wood should be at right angles to the long axis of the fiddle. It should not be of uniform thickness throughout its extent; but, on the contrary, ought to taper gradually from bottom to top, so as to be twice as thick below, where it rests upon the belly, as it is above, where it supports the strings. The holes in the bridge are not only ornamental, but serve an important purpose, in so far as they aid that particular conduction of vibrations, which is most suitable. These cuttings were fixed, after many trials, by Stradivari.

DIFFERENT PARTS AND ADJUNCTS OF A VIOLIN. 43

It has been suggested that the use of them is to sift, so to speak, the vibrations caused by the vibrating strings, so that only those, or mainly those, pass to the feet which are best adapted for the purpose of setting the body of the instrument vibrating.

With regard to the position of the bridge, the notches in the *f*-holes usually serve as a trustworthy guide, since they mark the situation which is correct in the case of each violin. This varies relatively to the build of each instrument, but, speaking generally, the bridge should be placed so that its posterior surface is 2⅜ inches distant from the interior extremity of the finger-board. The superior surface of the bridge should curve very slightly downwards towards that side of the fiddle, which is situated towards the right of the violinist when engaged in playing. The rounding of the bridge should conform exactly to that of the finger-board, and the bridge should be cut at the top, so as to form such a curve as will admit of the strings being at equal heights above the finger-board. Both bridge and finger-board must be neither too round nor too flat. If they are too round, the G and E strings will be too far from the reach of the bow. If, on the contrary, they are too flat, the bow will be liable, when playing on one string, to touch an adjoining one at the same time. Again, if the upper surface of the bridge is too flat, the finger-board being rounded, the G and E strings will be, of course, too high. An easy pressure of the finger-tips upon these strings will thus be insufficient to bring them down into contact with the finger-board. In this connection it may be remarked that the grooves in the nut of the finger-board must not be worn away, since it is necessary that the open strings may vibrate, without touching one another or the finger-board.

The strings must be situated in such a manner, that no difficulty will be experienced by a good player in the avoidance of other strings, when passing the bow on any open or stopped string.

The distance between the strings must be practically

HOW TO PLAY THE FIDDLE.

equal, and they must not be so close together that the fingers when touching one will touch another also, nor so close that one string when vibrating will touch the finger used for stopping a neighbouring string. Room must be allowed for the vibration of the strings both transversely and vertically.

Again, the bridge should incline very slightly backwards. When we come to the method of stringing, we shall see that the bridge must be thus inclined during the process of tightening the strings, and that it should not be pulled up by the increasing tension of the strings, so that it becomes perfectly perpendicular.

If the tone of a violin is not sufficiently strong, full, and powerful, matters may be slightly improved in many cases by the use of a bridge made of hard wood; while if it is not mellow and sweet in quality, soft wood should be selected as the material of which the bridge is to be composed.

The strings should not be so wide apart as to prevent or render difficult double stopping, where one finger has to do duty for two adjacent strings.

C. A Word on the Pegs, the Mute, the Resin, and the Finger-board.

The Pegs.—The pegs are made of ebony, or boxwood, or rose-wood. They should be firmly fixed into the holes made to receive them, so that when turned they will not slip. When smooth and polished with constant turning, they should be taken out, and rubbed with chalk and lead-pencil. Some use resin for this purpose; but it is a very great mistake to do so. The pegs should not taper too much. In case they are worn out or spoiled, or for any reason unsuitable, a new set should be at once obtained. They should be fitted at a violin-shop, since there it is well known how to do this quickly, easily, and well; but if one wishes, for any reason, to do it one's self, it is best to scrape them with a file at

DIFFERENT PARTS AND ADJUNCTS OF A VIOLIN. 43

first and afterwards with sand-paper, until they are of the right size. Care must be taken to file them evenly. At first even when well and carefully filed, some annoyance may be caused by the slipping of the pegs; but after a time they become suitably accommodated by use. We would here remark that the E-string fits into the bottom peg on the right hand-side of the neck, the A-string into the peg above it, the D-string into the top peg on the left-hand side of the neck, and the G-string into the bottom peg on the same side.

The *Mute* is an instrument used for subduing the tone of the violin. The terms *con sordino* and *senza sordino* are used respectively as directions for putting on and taking off the mute.

It is somewhat difficult for the player to fix and unfix his mute, while playing, without breaking the time. In order to obviate this difficulty, M. Vuillaume, in 1867, constructed the *sourdine pedale*, or "chin-mute," which, by the pressure of the chin upon the tail-piece of the fiddle, brings the mute into immediate connection with the bridge. When the pressure is removed, the mute is taken off.

The *Resin* must neither be too soft nor too brittle.

A special preparation of resin, in which oil is one of the ingredients, is sold in the violin-shops. It is nicely fitted into a small hollow wooden trough open at each end, so that the bow can be rubbed up and down on it. Messrs. Hill, 38, New Bond Street, and Messrs. Chanot, of Wardour Street, sell a very suitable article. Be sparing in the use of resin.

Many beginners within a week rub a large amount of resin upon the bow, or at any rate go so far as to make a decided groove in the resin. They delight to see the hair as white as snow, and to watch the particles falling upon the belly of the violin. Now, there is no need for this. It must be remembered that the tone of even a good violin becomes harsh with the use of too much resin. The particles of resin lodge in little lumps in the interstices of the hairs, and an intolerable harshness is the result. At the same time, it must be borne in mind that a want of resin is equally objectionable. The use of the resin is to enable the bow to bite the strings easily and smoothly throughout. An absence of resin will often cause a cessation of sound. This may be proved by passing a new bow on which no resin has been rubbed over the strings, when no sound at all is emitted. Thus resin should be used, but sparingly. Half a dozen passes of the bow over the resin are quite sufficient for a few hours' playing. With regard to the quality of the resin, that is best which is least brittle. That which is good for medical purposes may not be equally good for the bow. Practice will enable the beginner soon to know how much resin and what kind to use. The proper kind of resin may be bought at the shop of any good violin-dealer.

The *Finger-board* should be perfectly smooth and exactly rounded with the correct curve, since accurate stopping of the notes depends to a large extent on its surface being true. It is impossible, for instance, to stop fifths in tune on a rough or uneven finger-board.

Messrs. Hill, of 38, New Bond Street, sell a special preparation for rubbing the pegs, which is far superior to chalk and lead pencil. The same firm also sell a useful resin-holder in which the resin is exposed when a spring is pressed. When the pressure is released, the resin is enclosed and kept from dust and moisture. This is Hill and Hollyer's patent.

CHAPTER VI.

THE STRINGS AND THE METHOD OF ADJUSTING THEM PROPERLY.

A. THE STRINGS.

THE quality of the sound produced by a vibrating string, that is, the mode or manner of its vibration, depends partly on its density and degree of elasticity, and partly also on the way in which its movements are excited. In the cases of the piano, harp, guitar and

THE STRINGS AND THE METHOD OF STRINGING.

zither, the vibrations of the strings are produced by striking or plucking, whereas in the bowed instruments, such as the violin and violoncello, the bow is employed for this purpose. The violin-strings give tones which possess great brilliancy owing to the high upper partials which are constituents of them. At the same time, these high-pitched components are quickly damped, and thus a metallic character of sound is prevented.

Not only does a string vibrate as a whole, whereby the prime or fundamental tone is produced, but in addition its fractional parts also vibrate, in some sense independently, thus giving rise to the "upper partials." Half the string vibrates, giving the octave, and so on.

The strings of a violin are not merely stretched over the resonance-box; but their direction is altered by passing over a bridge on which they press with great force.

The degree of thickness of the strings which is best depends on the temperament and build of the violin, and in some cases it is wise to select strings which are most suitable to the fingers. The Italian strings are the best. Of these, the Roman are very hard, brilliant, and slightly rough; the Neapolitan are smoother, softer, whiter, but not so good as Roman strings; while the Paduan are highly polished and strong, but frequently false. The French E-strings are brittle. The German are too strongly bleached, and hence faulty in sound. The best and strongest strings are made of the intestines of spring lambs killed in September: and the superiority of Italian strings is partly to be attributed to the climate, for in Italy the sun does what has to be done artificially in more northern regions. Hence it happens that since the demand for the intestines of the September lambs is far greater than the supply, there is always a large number of inferior strings in the market. Moreover, although a high price must be paid for the best strings; yet the fact that a large sum is demanded is not a sufficient guarantee of good quality.

Still it is necessary to use always the best strings

that can be procured. It will be found to be economical to use the best, as strings vary as much in quality as in price. Really good strings, when opened out, should exhibit very nearly as much power of recoil as a watch-spring. A G-string covered with silver wire is better and cheaper in the end than a copper-covered one, although the latter can be obtained for twopence, and the former costs from one to two shillings. A string covered with copper wire soon becomes coated with verdigris, and the tone produced by it when in this state, is, as might be expected, bad. It is, moreover, not only the covering, which is better, in the silver-covered strings. As a matter of fact, the whole string is of superior quality, and lasts far longer. At the same time, owing to the fact that a copper covered G, is thicker than a silver covered one, the former will bear much more pressure. The latter, on account of being thin, gives out a harsh scratchy tone, if the bow is pressed hard upon it. Hence it is, that if only the copper G is carefully preserved, it is in the above respect more suitable than the silver one. It is also stated by some authorities that the silver and copper strings, are suited respectively to different kinds of violins. The E-string should be of the best Roman or Neapolitan gut. The Acrabelle is greatly disliked by some, and its tone is certainly inferior; but others prefer it on account of its greater durability, and because it is not so easily damaged by the perspiration from the fingers. The use of a silk string or of a wire for the first string is a great mistake. It should be borne in mind that the Acrabelle does not stretch so much as the other strings, and that consequently the required pitch is obtained with a much slighter twist of the peg than is required in the case of the Roman or Neapolitan strings. The E-string should be quite transparent and clear, for if opaque it will usually produce a bad tone. The A and D strings are never very clear, since they are spun with several threads; but, as the E-strings are never composed of more than a few threads, absence of transparency in them denotes inferior material. Sometimes a string is found to yield a double sound. In this case it must

THE STRINGS AND THE METHOD OF STRINGING. 49

be removed at once, and another must be used. It is a practice with some violinists to rub a bow with resin on it along the length of new strings, across that part of them which is used. This is said to make the bow bite the strings at once.

With regard to the selection of strings, one should try to find those which are most suitable to the instrument, *i.e.*, to choose those which are of the thickness and quality which will give rise to the greatest ease, roundness, and freedom of tone. Secondly, it is requisite that the strings should give good fifths—a matter somewhat dependent on the shape of the fingers, and on the cut of the finger-board, but also on the relative thickness of the strings. Thirdly, false strings must be avoided. Much caution is required in the case of the E-strings. The method of detection recommended by Spohr is to hold tightly the string at each end, between the thumb and forefinger of each hand, and to make it vibrate by giving it a jerk. If only two lines are seen, the string is considered to be true; if three, it is deemed false. This mode of decision is said to be useful, but in the case of the A and D strings it may be misleading, since the lines are frequently not very definite. If the strings are actually put on, they can, of course, be easily tested by the ear. It is important to recollect that tone, although it depends a great deal upon the quality of the violin, is nevertheless influenced to a considerable extent by the nature of the strings. Thus a good G-string, which has been used for two or three months, acquires a much better tone than it had at first. This holds, too, with regard to the other strings. Sometimes, however, an Acrabelle E-string lasts for about a month, and then, instead of improving, seems to lose all purity of tone. In that case the sooner it is taken off the better. It is necessary to have each string of the same thickness throughout, and for testing this the guage made for the purpose is to be recommended. Its cost is but a trifle.

Strings should be wrapped up carefully in a piece of oiled silk and kept in an air-tight tin box: but it is advisable not to buy a large stock. Two D's and A's half a dozen E's, and two G's will suffice. Care is especially needed with regard to the preservation of the G-strings, as they are easily tarnished and spoiled by exposure to the air and to moisture. Another point with regard to the preservation of strings is to keep them from becoming dry. One cannot be too careful about the preservation of violin-strings.

B. The Mode of Stringing.

As a rule, one string as sold in the shops is long enough to make two for the violin, and should therefore be cut in half. The E-strings will sometimes admit of being divided into three parts, the A's and D's into two. The G-string can only be used as a whole. In order to fasten a string, take one of the halves, tie a knot near the end (in the case of all but the E-string), place it through the proper hole in the tail-piece, and pull the string firmly, so that the knot will become placed at the superior extremity of the hole and point downwards. It is well to bear in mind that the string must be properly handled, otherwise a *kink* may be produced, which tends to derange its particles: and thus spoil the tone of the string. Attention should also be given to this point when unwinding the coil. The coil is generally fastened together by very thin pieces of red catgut. In cutting these off, be careful not to cut the string itself at the same time, as the very slight *notch* thus made will spoil the tone-power of the string. Having fixed the string into the tail-piece with the knot downwards, place the peg in the hole made for it in the neck of the violin. Take now the other end of the string, and insert it upwards into the hole in the peg, which is already fixed in the neck. Twist the peg round, in order to make the end of the string rise out of the neck, so as to enable you to take hold of the end. In some violins the peg into which the A-string has to be inserted lies so close up to the scroll, that it is necessary to use a small

THE STRINGS AND THE METHOD OF STRINGING.

pair of tweezers in order to get between one's fingers the end of the string. Having now taken hold of the end of the string, draw it underneath the portion of the same string which is stretched, and then pull it up close to the peg, so as to make a half-knot. Hold it tightly with the left hand, screwing up the peg at the same time, until the string is properly stretched for the required pitch. Although it is very difficult to describe the mode of stringing, it is very easy to show it practically. Any violin-seller will be able to explain it fully. Take care in putting in a string that it does not cross or touch another string, otherwise in the process of screwing up the peg, it will draw up the other string as well, thus pitching not only the string which is intended to be stretched, but the other string also, which is already pitched. We speak from direful experience. On one occasion having pitched the A-string, I put on a new D-string. The D creased and pressed on the A, so that by screwing up the *D-peg* both strings were thus tightened. I could not tell what was the matter, and how it was that I could not make my D one-fifth with my A. The fact of the case was the A was being stretched along with the D. At last I discovered my mistake, and have not since forgotten it.

The E-string must not be fastened by means of a knot, as it generally snaps, if a knot be used. It should be actually tied into the hole at the tail-piece. The E-string does not last so long as the other strings, even if it be an Acrabelle. It generally snaps near the bridge. Indeed, the D and A strings also break in this part; but, long before this happens, it may be observed that the fibres of which they are composed have become untwisted. In this case take them off at once, and put on new strings. Sometimes a string breaks suddenly in a weak part, as soon as it is brought up to the correct pitch. If the string is not frayed, and if the other parts of it are in good order, the sound portion of it may be utilised again. Half an E-string is, as a rule, several inches longer than is required, and therefore will admit of being thus manipulated. The D and A strings, especially the former, generally last so long that it is not advisable to utilise the sound part of them again. Indeed, one-half is only just long enough for the purpose required. The G-string is made of the right length, so that it cannot be used again. When once broken, it is spoiled; but the tension required in the case of this string is so small that it will last for a long time—a year, or even more.

When stringing, take care that the bridge is always upright: but in screwing up the pegs, especially when new strings are being put on, cause the bridge to incline slightly towards the tail-piece. As the strings are being stretched, they will draw the bridge along with them into the upright position; so that if it were in the first instance placed so as to be perpendicular to the long axis of the fiddle, it would, when the strings were stretched be drawn so as to incline towards the finger-board by reason of the strain on the strings. Moreover, if the strings require to be greatly stretched, the bridge may fall down and snap asunder, and even the belly of the violin may be broken at the same time. This point is of some importance, as much time, trouble, and expense may be saved by attention to it. With careful treatment a bridge should last for years; though it is frequently the case that beginners destroy a large number, simply owing to a wrong method of stringing their instruments. It is the custom among some players to stretch their strings before putting them on the violin, by placing the foot on one end of the string, and pulling the other end with the hand. This practice is to be condemned, as the strings may thus be spoiled.

CHAPTER VII.

THE BOW AND BOWING.

A. The Bow

THE possessor of a fine violin has no easy task in procuring a bow most suitably adapted to produce the highest quality of tone from his instrument. The hair should be fairly slack, but firm and even. It will in that case bend more freely over the string, and more effectually alter the relation of the velocity of the string during the rebound, to that of the string while clinging to the hair of the bow. This would seem to affect the relative force of the constituent upper partial tones, thus modifying the quality of the tone produced. It is only the best violins which allow of a powerful motion of the strings without producing a roughness of tone. In fact, the more perfect a fiddle is, the more energetically it may be bowed without a diminution of purity in the sounds produced. The tension of the hair, the elasticity and the lightness of the stick, are all important factors.

· Although the violins of Amati, Stradivari, and the old masters are still regarded as the finest ever made, the bows of modern days are undoubtedly the best. From the time of Corelli constant changes have been made in the form of the bow; and its length has been increased, until it has at last been brought, in great part by the labours of Francis Tourte, of Paris, to its present high state of perfection.

He lived from 1775 to 1835, and improved the bow about as much as Stradivari did the violin itself. In the absence of bows shaped according to his ideas, delicate shades of *piano* and *forte* execution would be impossible. By making the bow curve inwards, he made it possible to combine great strength with elasticity and lightness. He fixed the length of the stick, and arranged the construction so that the centre of gravity is placed with the view of making the bow capable of being easily balanced.

The superiority of modern bows is as fully recognized as is that of old violins. Up to about the year 1650 the bow was short and clumsy, somewhat like our double-bass bows. Tartini improved it by making it thinner, longer, and more elastic, and especially by constructing it so that the concavity of the stick turned away from the hair and not towards it. When buying a bow, the beginner must remember that forgery is not uncommon in regard to bows. The length of a modern bow from one extreme point to another is twenty-nine inches.

Let us now consider the make of this most important though simple-looking instrument of compression and friction. The bow consists of a long stick or rod, into one part of which, called the head, one end of a thick hank of horsehair is fastened by a kind of wedge or plug. The other end of the hair is held in a similar way, by means of a piece of ebony called the *nut*, which is connected by means of a screw arrangement with the stick, in such a way that the hair can be tightened or relaxed at will. The number of hairs is from about 100 to 250. The kinds of wood used for making bows are Brazil-wood, snake-wood, iron-wood, and log-wood.

It is advisable for the beginner to provide himself with a really good bow as well as with a good violin. The ordinary bows, sold for about half a crown or three shillings, are of inferior make, and are apt, when freely used, to dance upon the strings, as it were, especially when one is playing rapid passages. In a good bow, the hair, when tight, should come nearest to the middlemost portion of the stick. The hair should be sufficiently broad : and the separate hairs should be close together and equally stretched. If some hairs are observed to be lying loose when the others are tense, they should be removed, and care should be taken to clip each one off at its extreme ends.

The quality of the bow as a whole depends principally on the character and make of the woodwork, nut and screw; while the arrangement of the hair depends on the carefulness or carelessness of the person who fits it. Naturally, however, one always finds the hair most perfectly arranged in the best bows. The cost of fitting a fresh hank is always one shilling, whether the bow originally cost one guinea or half a crown. Nicety in the arrangement of the hair is most readily obtained in the best bows, owing to the fact that their ends are better constructed for exerting a tight hold. Always take care, when buying a bow or when getting fresh hair fitted, to insist upon a proper arrangement of the hair. A good bow cannot be procured for less than a guinea. It is a great mistake to begin with a half-crown bow. If one wishes to study the violin properly, it is requisite to have a good bow at the outset. Two, or three, or even five guineas may be given for a bow; but a sufficiently good one may be obtained for one guinea. Some bows made by Vuillaume, of Paris, are furnished with cylindrical nippers, which can be separated at pleasure. These are to be preferred to the ordinary ones, inasmuch as the equal stretching of the hairs, can be thereby more easily obtained, and the player himself may fit in a new hank of hair when required.

Hollow steel bows are used by some persons and preferred by them, but it is not clear that they possess any special excellence. With regard to the preservation of the bow, take care not to handle it roughly. Do not touch the horsehair with the fingers, for there is generally some perspiration on them, which may settle on the bow and cause it when being used to give forth a scratching or a squeaking sound. It is necessary to avoid exposing the bow to the heat of the sun or to that of a fire, as the resin would thereby be melted on the hairs, and the woodwork would become more or less damaged. Some players never seem to know how much the hair is to be stretched, and, while some have it too slack, others have it too greatly tightened, so that both hair and woodwork are in a state of the utmost tension. Now, both extremes are to be avoided. Too great a tension gives rise to a harsh sound, and is apt to break the hair. If, however, the hairs be too loose, when the bow is drawn along the string, the sound will be at times interrupted. When the bow is properly stretched, there is the space of half an inch between the hair and the bow at the middle point; and in good bows this point, the exact centre of the bow, is that at which the hair and woodwork approach each other most closely. The desirability of having the bow fairly stretched, and not too slack, will be referred to again in our remarks on the method of using the bow. When the bow is not in use, the hair should be relaxed by loosening the screw, so that the strain upon the hairs may not be continuous. The case of the strings is different; for, while continued tension of the hair is liable to produce some effect upon the stick, tension of the strings does not damage any part of the violin. On the other hand there are great advantages in leaving the strings stretched as for playing. Some persons, however, relax all the strings of their violin, when it is not in use; while others loosen the E-string alone.

The strings are tuned to the correct pitch, and are thus ready at all times to be used for practice, if not loosened. They will often remain in perfect tune for a considerable time, and in most cases they require, at any rate, only a slight twist of the peg to bring them up to pitch. If, however, the strings are all loosened, either wholly or partially, a great deal of time and trouble must be wasted in order to bring them up to pitch, every time the violin is to be used. No benefit, in short, is derived from loosening the strings; but, on the other hand, decided disadvantages result.

B. Bowing.

1. *Method of holding the Bow.*—The first point to be learnt about bowing is the proper mode of handling the bow. Many beginners hold the bow either too daintily and lightly on the one hand, or too tightly and with great rigidity of the finger-joints on the other. It is of the greatest importance that the bow should be held firmly, but at the same time in such a manner as to preserve the greatest flexibility and elasticity of the finger-joints. One great mistake sometimes made is consciously or unconsciously to place the fingers upon the bow, at a place too far away from the nut. It is not uncommon to look upon the piece of covering on the stick of the bow, as indicating the exact spot where the fingers ought to be placed. So far do some carry out this idea that they have the silver wire taken off, and a piece of wash-leather or kid placed there instead. Some, indeed, have been known to use kid stuffed with cotton-wool, so as to form a kind of pad for the fingers, in order that the bow may not slip out of their grasp. Now, the fingers should be placed quite at the end of the bow close to the nut, and, according to many experienced players, the thumb should be placed quite inside the nut as far as possible. In this case the projecting piece of ebony, which is ornamental, perhaps, but not useful, should be cut away altogether, so as to allow free ingress to the thumb. Of course, the fingers are not to be crowded together; but due consideration must be paid to the proper intervals between them. The difficulty and awkwardness experienced by those who hold the bow at a point distant about an inch or more from the nut are very great, especially when they attempt to play rapid passages, or anything with execution. In double stopping, and in the playing of chords, the bow, when held in this way, is apt to swerve aside altogether from the grasp of the fingers. The principle on which the correct holding of the bow as above described depends, is the same as that which leads a man

in working a pump to grasp the knob or end of the pump handle, and to avoid placing his hands at a distance from the end. In fact, when holding the bow too far away from the nut, the violinist has very little power over it.

2. *Method of using the Bow* (a).— Use the bow always with the woodwork bent away from yourself, towards the finger-board. You will thus use, of course, only a few hairs of the bow, instead of all of them, and in this way a better tone will be produced than if the whole breadth of the hair—that is, if all the hairs are made to play upon the strings. Hence is seen the necessity for having the bow fairly tense; since otherwise the woodwork of the bow will touch and pass over the strings. In any case, when bowing strongly, if the horse hair is not fairly tense, the hairs might touch the stick, or the stick the strings; but the possibility of the latter occurring is increased when the bow is held as it ought to be held, namely, sideways towards the finger-board.

As the violin is inclined at an angle of about 45 degrees, it is well to take care that you do not scrape the woodwork of the violin with the bow, especially when playing on the E-string. The very slightest inclination of the bow out of the right line may give rise to this fault. Not only does the violin-player come to grief, in that when he ought to be playing a note, he omits one, on account of the bow being off the string, and scraping on the woodwork of the violin; but also the violin is damaged or rendered unsightly by the actual scraping away of the varnish, and eventually of the woodwork itself.

The way above described is, in our opinion, decidedly the best, but some violinists maintain that the bow must be laid so as to be quite flat on the strings, *i.e.*, so as to use all the hairs; while others advise that the entire breadth of the hair should be used for the beginning of a down-bow, and that there should be a gradual change to the side as the tip of the bow is approached; and that an up-bow should begin with the side and end with the whole surface.

(b) Observe, by the aid of the looking-glass, whether

you are making a straight bow, as it called, or not. In order to do this, draw the bow across the whole length from heel to point in a straight line.

To keep the bow always at right angles to the strings is more difficult of accomplishment than might at first sight appear; because what is really a straight stroke does not seem so to the player, and a curved or crooked stroke seems to be perfectly straight. The bow must be drawn apparently out of a parallel line with the bridge, but this apparent deviation from a line parallel with the bridge is not a real one. In returning the bow from tip to nut, bend or rather turn the wrist slightly. This will enable the bow to move in a straight line. Remember that all motion must proceed from the wrist and elbow, and not from the arm. The arm, on the contrary, must be comparatively still and motionless; but of course a slight motion of the arm is a necessity. Beginners almost always move the arm with great freedom, without even knowing that they are doing so. They suppose they are making a straight stroke when they are in reality either making a slanting stroke, or more probably describing a semicircular sweep of the bow over the string or strings. A tone thus produced is uncertain and variable as well as poor, and generally has a squeaking or scratching sound. Moreover, it so happens that this mode of playing presents a bad appearance to the eyes of onlookers.

In bowing, be careful rather to whip than to scrape since scraping checks the vibrations. A springing, elastic kind of bowing is desirable.

A fault generally committed by those who do not bow straight, is that they do not allow the bow to remain on one point on the strings. It wanders between the bridge and the end of the finger-board, then close to the bridge, then almost on the finger board. Now, as the *timbre* of the sound varies with the place struck, becomes harsher nearest the bridge, and less harsh away from the bridge; the consequence is we have an alteration of sound, a varying *timbre*. The effect, I need hardly say, is anything but pleasing.

(c) It is necessary that the pupil should firstly learn the

best mode of beginning the bowing. Each note should be made so as to sound evenly and smoothly from the very first. There should be no perceptible jerk at the commencement. This is a matter of some difficulty, and as a matter of fact very few amateurs begin nicely.

The avoidance of jerks is also a matter of great difficulty, when one is playing a note which extends over a bar or two. When a note should be held out for several bars, it is necessary, when one has reached one extremity of the bow, to return without breaking the continuity of the note. The bow should be passed more slowly, as one is using the portion of it which is near the end, and then without any jerk, an up-bow should be substituted for a down-bow, or *vice versa*. Thus there will be no perceptible break in playing a long-continued note. This should be practised continually until the player is able to do it without difficulty. Professional violinists spend a considerable time in the practice of this accomplishment alone.

(*d*) In double-stopping, great care should be taken that the bow should actually touch both strings evenly throughout. Most beginners find a difficulty in doing this. They commence with the bow evenly laid on both strings, but as they come towards either extremity of the bow they inadvertently (perhaps through weakness of the wrist, as might arise from undue smoking, or other indulgence) fail to cause the bow to touch both strings at once. A very slight movement of the wrist is sufficient to cause the bow to touch only one string.

(*e*) Sometimes two notes have to be played in succession either by an up-bow, or with a downward stroke of the bow. In this case it is necessary to avoid jerking, though the staccato playing might represent to the beginner the idea of jerking. It should be borne in mind that an up-stroke or a down-stroke of the bow may be divided into separate movements without jerks, and it is necessary in some passages to use this method. *A propos* of this, we may remark that the same passage may, on the violin, be played in many different ways with regard to bowing.

THE BOW AND BOWING.

If in *piano* passages the bow is used a little further from the bridge, the tone is not only less loud, but is also rendered more dull. This is owing to the fact that the fifth or the sixth partial tone which aids in imparting brightness will not be present. Similar alterations in quality can be produced by using different bows.

(*f*) The following is from the celebrated Guiseppe Tartini. "Your first study should be the manner of holding, balancing, and pressing the bow lightly but steadily upon the strings, in such a manner that it shall seem to *breathe* the first tone it gives, which must proceed from the friction of the string, not from percussion, as by a blow given with a hammer upon it. This depends upon laying the bow lightly upon the strings at the first contact, and on gently pressing it afterwards. If this is done gradually, there can scarcely be too much force given to it; because if the tone is begun with delicacy there is little danger of rendering it afterwards either coarse or harsh. To practise this smooth bowing, first exercise yourself in a swell upon an open string. Begin *pianissimo*, and increase the tone by slow degrees to *fortissimo*. Do this with both up and down bow. After this, in order to acquire that bright pulsation and play of the wrist whence velocity in bowing arises, it will be best for you to practise every day one of the allegros, of which there are three, in Corelli's solos, which entirely move in semiquavers. The first is in D, in playing which you should accelerate the motion a little each time, till you arrive at the greatest degree of swiftness possible. The notes should be played staccato, *i.e.*, separate and detached. Play first with the point of the bow, then with that part which is between the point and the middle, then with the middle of the bow. Begin the allegros or flights sometimes with an up-bow and sometimes with a down-bow."

Young violinists must recognise that a very great deal depends on the method of using the bow, and that scratching and other errors can only be avoided by much painstaking practice in the use of the bow-arm.

CHAPTER VIII.

THE METHOD OF TUNING THE VIOLIN.

> "How sweet the moonlight sleeps upon this bank!
> Here will we sit, and let the sounds of music
> Creep in our ears: soft stillness, and the night,
> Become the touches of sweet harmony.
> Sit, Jessica: look how the floor of heaven
> Is thick inlaid with patines of bright gold.
> There's not the smallest orb which thou behold'st,
> But in his motion like an angel sings,
> Still quiring to the young-eyed cherubims:
> Such harmony is in immortal souls;
> But whilst this muddy vesture of decay
> Doth grossly close it in, we cannot hear it."
>
> *Merchant of Venice.*

THE violinist, unlike the pianist, is expected to be able to tune the instrument used. It is consequently of the greatest importance that the learner should pay attention to this matter. Nothing can be more injurious for a beginner than to practise his scales and exercises upon a violin which is out of tune. Indeed, it should be in perfect tune. The person who neglects this fundamental rule is sure to gain gradually an incorrect idea of pitch, even if previously a tolerably correct one was possessed. The difficulty of tuning the violin is somewhat great at first. Annoyance may result from the slipping of the pegs from turning them too far, and so on, so that one may feel inclined to let imperfect fifths and chords do duty for perfect ones. It is possible by judging proportion of distance, to play correctly on a violin which is not properly tuned; but this mode of playing, even when possible, should only be resorted to when the pegs slip during a public performance. Here, again, the primary importance of having a good instru-

THE METHOD OF TUNING THE VIOLIN.

ment is obvious. In inferior ones it is next to impossible to prevent the pegs from slipping, in spite of every precaution, the reason being that the wood and workmanship of the neck and the peg-holes are defective. Many beginners have, in consequence of such vexations, after a few months' practice, given up violin-playing altogether in disgust. When a violin is in perfect tune, there are fixed distances between the points at which the fingers must be placed for the production of the different notes; and to be obliged to alter those distances tends to confuse and to bewilder the learner. It is, in fact, exceedingly difficult even for experienced players to do this: *a propos* of this matter, it should be borne in mind that children ought not to begin with violins of small size. To recommend them to do so is a very great mistake, to which we can bear witness by experience. Having spent almost fruitlessly a considerable period of time on such a toy, and having had to unlearn all the distances learned with some labour, one is able to speak very feelingly and positively. Mr. Haweis, an eminent authority, in his work entitled "My Musical Life," draws attention to this matter (vol i. p. 19).

The instrument must be in perfect tune. In order to tune it correctly, the novice might think it well to adjust all the strings in point of pitch to that of the corresponding notes of the piano. In this way, of course, the violin could not be perfectly tuned, inasmuch as the piano is not tuned so as to produce perfect fifths. In most cases, too, the piano itself is not in perfect tune, even according to the method adopted; unless, indeed, it has recently been set in order by a good pianoforte-tuner. Now, the violin, on the contrary, must be tuned so as to give perfect fifths. The proper way to do this, is to adjust the pitch of the A-string by means of an A tuning-fork. If, however, one is playing with a pianoforte accompaniment, the pitch of this string must be determined by that of the note corresponding to it on the piano. In all cases the rest of the strings on the violin must be tuned independently of the piano. Having then made the A-string yield a note of the right pitch, whether it be concert pitch or that of the piano in question, the E-string is to be stretched so as to make a perfect fifth with A. The D-string must then be adjusted so that it makes a perfect fifth with A. Lastly, the G-string is tuned until it gives with D a perfect fifth. A crisp frosty sound of unusual brilliancy may be said to be characteristic of a perfect fifth.

The difference between absolute and relative pitch is also to be noted. The absolute pitch of a note is the actual number of vibrations per second of which it is composed, without regard to the number of which any other note is compounded.

The relative pitch of a note is measured by the proportion which the number of vibrations composing it bears to that of some other note, usually the tonic or key-note.

A violinist playing with the accompaniment of different pianos has to *alter* the absolute pitch of his violin, but to preserve carefully the exact proportion between the pitch of the four strings. With regard to accurate tuning, it may be said that there is always something unpleasing to a person who possesses a good ear for music, in any imperfect chord or fifth.

This unpleasantness arises from the beats, which may be said to produce upon one who is musical an effect similar to that which a flickering light causes to persons of sensitive eyesight. The presence or absence of beats serves as the chief guide to the tuner. It is well-known that, when tuning pianofortes on the system called that of equal temperament, the tuner, who is making his intervals swerve aside very slightly from strict accuracy, has absolutely nothing else to guide him except the number of beats which his flattened or sharpened interval makes, and that, starting with a perfect third or fifth, he flattens or sharpens his interval by exactly the number of beats required. We must here bear in mind with regard to beats that the two tones which, when sounding together, give rise to beats, are really due to two sets of vibrations, of which one set travels more quickly than the other. The varying rates bring about at regular intervals, firstly, an augmen-

THE METHOD OF TUNING THE VIOLIN.

tation of sound, when the crests of the two waves correspond; and, secondly a diminution of sound, when the crest of one wave corresponds with the trough of the other." (Some of the above is taken from the Student's Helmholtz (Broadhouse), but slightly altered).

Every violinist must learn the sounds of perfect fifths and of perfect chords, so that he can be absolutely certain as to whether his instrument is properly tuned, not only when tuning it, but also while playing upon it. The tuning-fork cannot be dispensed with. The A-string may, and in fact generally does, gradually slacken. The peg, too, may slide or slip, and thus, of course, the note produced by this loosened string becomes flat. Now, as above observed, the player takes this note A as his standard of pitch, tuning the other strings in relation to it, so that it is quite possible that the violinist who never tests his A-string with the aid of a tuning-fork, may find his violin has become very flat, lower by a note or even more, than it ought to be. Even if this lowness of pitch was not *in itself* objectionable, as being out of proportion to recognised standards, it must yet be remembered that the brilliancy of tone of the violin depends to a large extent upon a certain definite pitch being preserved. The violin-strings must be kept at almost concert pitch, since the violin-box is adapted in point of resonance to certain notes, and also because each string requires a certain amount of tension, in order to give out a proper sound at all. In the violoncello a fine tone can be produced with low notes which on the violin would be dull and toneless. A G-string on the violin may be slackenad so as to give the same note as a higher string on the 'cello; but while the tone produced by the former would be very bad, that of the latter would be good. Thus a certain tension is required in order to produce a good tone. Now, many beginners do not observe this rule; but, on the contrary, become accustomed to playing at a low pitch. A nasal, formless, and uncertain tone is the result. They wonder at the brilliancy of the tone of other violins, forgetting that their own instrument is too low in pitch to give out any brilliancy. It is, then, best to keep the instrument at concert pitch. Hence there is a necessity, except when playing with the pianoforte accompaniment, for the use of the tuning-fork; unless, indeed, one has an exact remembrance of the required pitch, which can only be acquired by very long practice.

Great attention must be paid to the following point, otherwise one will never, even with the greatest accuracy of ear, be able to tune a violin properly. Many persons turn the pegs either too far or not far enough. This tendency may soon be avoided with practice and care; but there is a more serious difficulty to be mentioned. Many, when they have turned the peg sufficiently, instead of sending it home into its socket or hole, involuntarily give it an extra twist, thus imparting to the string a pitch which is higher than it should be, by the fraction of a note. In this case, although the string, when the peg was first turned, was in tune; still, when the peg is sent home, the string is out of tune. A similar fault may be observed often enough in rifle practice. Many a novice adjusts his rifle with tolerable accuracy for the bull's-eye: but, just at the moment of pressing the trigger, there may be a tendency to draw the rifle involuntarily towards the right and upwards. The trigger is, in short, pulled sideways, instead of being simply pressed. The consequence is that the mark cannot be hit, even though the man may be in other respects an accurate marksman, so long as this fault is unaltered. Instead, therefore, of hitting the bull's-eye, a centre, or more probably an outer is made. Very often he misses the target altogether. With regard to the violin, let the peg be fixed immediately after it has been sufficiently turned. Drive it home straight as a bolt, avoiding the unconscious twist, and taking care to do it quietly and without a jerk, just as a gentleman would pass a glass of wine to a lady.

We might here mention that when a string is pitched a fraction of a note too high, it may often be reduced to the proper pitch by a slight pull with the fingers.

Before closing this short chapter, we would again lay special stress on the absolute necessity of always having the violin in perfect tune. Some beginners find so much trouble and difficulty in tuning that they are apt to grow careless in this matter. Let this rule be ever in your mind: When playing, always take care that your fiddle is in perfect tune.

CHAPTER IX.

SOME RULES TO BE OBSERVED IN PLAYING.

THE following rules are of great importance, some of them are based upon the practical teaching of violinists and most of them are the result of much thought and practical experience on our part. They are formulated with a view to meet those difficulties which appear most seriously to beset the learner. At the outset, it may be said, by way of encouragement, that nothing can be more difficult at first than to pay attention to a large number of rules. While observing one, a beginner is apt to forget another; but there is no reason for discouragement or anxiety in the person who really makes up the mind conscientiously and thoroughly to strive, and keep on striving. After a time, unconsciously almost, the habit of attention to all rules will be gained. In this matter the beginner will receive help from the fact that the non-observance of any one rule will always show itself either in faulty playing, or by an extreme difficulty in the maintenance of good execution. Some people there are who play very fairly, and yet break a great many rules; but they always play with more or less difficulty and constraint, and are uncertain in their performances. For instance, many amateur violin-players scarcely ever draw the bow in a direction exactly at right angles with the strings. Now these persons frequently complain very much of the tone of their instrument, even though the violin be a good one. One may hear observations such as the following: "I can't imagine how it is. My instrument is very bad in tone to-day. It varies greatly in tone. Sometimes its tone is good, and sometimes squeaky." The answer in many cases is that it is their mode of playing which is at fault, and not the instrument. Bad workmen generally find fault with their tools.

1. In all cases and at all times, for the first year of practice at least, the beginner should play so that he can see himself in a looking-glass. The learner should stand or sit with the right side of the body facing the glass. This is to be strongly recommended for various reasons. In the first place, it is for the purpose of preventing the making of grimaces. In singing, pianoforte-playing, and more especially in violin-playing, the contortions of the facial muscles give rise to the making of wry faces, which are liable to excite the risible feelings of the spectators. Moreover, one will be enabled to see whether the following rules are being carried out or not. Of course, a tutor will tell the learner how the fiddle and bow are being held, and how the fingering is being done; but as a great part of the practice needed must necessarily be done at home by one's self alone, it is well to have a means of judging whether the mode of playing be correct or incorrect.

2. The learner should stand in an upright, erect position. The body should be held easily, and not stiffly, and its weight should rest as much as possible on the left foot. The right foot must be placed a little to the right, and a little forward, and it should be situated so as to make a slight angle with the left foot. Thus for the left side stability is secured, whereby the violin can be firmly grasped, while for the right side that freedom is ensured which is necessary for the proper handling of the bow." (Altered from Courvoiseur). Whether you sit or stand, let the position of the body be easy, and not constrained. Sit or stand upright, and do not stoop. Lean very slightly forwards, and certainly not backwards.

3. The scroll of the violin should be held so that it neither slopes downwards nor rises upwards; but in a perfectly horizontal or level position, so as to be immediately opposite the left side of the lower jaw, and a little to the

SOME RULES TO BE OBSERVED IN PLAYING.

left of the point of the left shoulder. The head of the player should be inclined slightly downwards towards the left side, while the right side of the violin should be held so as to slope downwards towards the right side. It should be tilted downwards, in fact, just so much as to form an angle of forty-five degrees with the horizontal plane. This downward inclination to the right side is for the purpose of avoiding the brushing of the woodwork of the fiddle with the bow, while one is playing on the E-string, and also in order to enable the player with ease and facility to reach the G-string. The instrument should just touch the left jaw rather than the chin, and the jaw is not to be pressed down upon it in order to hold it. The chin must not actually grasp the instrument, but the chin, or, better still, the left side of the lower jaw, should lightly rest upon it. Although at first sight it would perhaps appear that Joachim grasps his violin tightly with the left jaw, this is said not to be the case. On the contrary, he holds the instrument lightly, delicately, but at the same time with great firmness. When the grip of the instrument by the jaw is unnecessarily firm, the nerves of the players face are set in an unusual degree of vibration. The hairs of the face also vibrate, and if the skin is sensitive, irritation of it results. These annoyances tend to distract the attention of the violinist, and thereby cause faulty playing. It is our conviction that a tight grip of the instrument tends to stop the vibrations and thus spoil the tone, and we also hold that chin-rests have probably a similar bad effect. Chin-rests are useful for some, especially for those who are unfortunate enough to possess what is usually called a double chin. They should be avoided unless absolutely necessary. To those who are either compelled or determined to use one, the flat fretted ones are to be recommended as being the best. Never move the violin along the bow. Some do this partially. The instrument should be kept exactly in its right position.

4. The music must be placed on a stand, so that it can be seen without stooping. If the player stoops, the

violin is necessarily held so as to slope downwards and the bow may then slip or slide off the strings. On the other hand, do not have the music too high. If the music is too greatly elevated, the violin will also be held too high, and there will be a tendency to hold the head and shoulders too far backwards, and if sitting, the player will probably assume a position of ease, like that of lying too comfortably in an arm-chair. It would be well when sitting to use a suitable stool, and *not a chair*, since one is apt in a chair to sit too comfortably. Avoid the practice of holding the violin against the chest, instead of against the jaw. Many are tempted to do this. It is impossible to play properly with the violin held in this position, although many street-players adopt this method, apparently not without some success.

It has been discovered, no doubt by experience, that the proper manipulation of the instrument depends upon holding it up to the jaw. However, with some amount of difficulty and by long practice, I conceive that the violin might be played on, if held in a lower position. The great difficulty in this point consists in manipulating with ease and dexterity the *notes* at the extreme ends of the strings. Supposing, however, that it were possible to play the instrument in this manner, there is one great advantage which would result, viz., the tone would be heard with more accuracy and distinctness by the players. It is for this reason, perhaps, that it is so much easier to test the tone of a violin when played by another person than when played by one's self. The tone of the instrument when held in the normal position strikes too loudly upon the auditory apparatus.

Talking of street-players reminds me of a fraud sometimes practised. You may see in the street or elsewhere two men, each provided with a fiddle, one of whom is playing more or less beautifully in the orthodox manner, while the other places his fiddle in all kinds of positions, over his head, behind his back, and so on. His vagaries will probably be fantastic in the extreme, and all the while he is supposed to be playing the same piece as his com-

SOME RULES TO BE OBSERVED IN PLAYING. 71

cade, whereas in reality he is not playing at all. He is only shamming.

This reminds me of another incident which I recollect reading. At an evening concert two gentlemen had arranged to play a duet with trombones. Each fell ill, and each, therefore, provided a substitute, who, instead of playing, should content himself with watching his colleague, and imitating his movements. The result may be imagined. When their turn came, the two substitutes sat down gravely, and began watching each other. At last one of them, more venturous than his friend, noticing signs of impatience on the part of the audience and of distress on the part of his fellow, whom he imagined to be merely nervous at the beginning, opened out his instrument. What was his astonishment on having done this, when he found his friend doing exactly the same, and then stopping short! In each case no sound was produced, as each had been instructed to content himself merely with outward signs of playing. Confusion and dismay fell upon them both, and at length they both made a precipitate and ignominious exit. "Are you not the celebrated Mr. Brown?" "No, I'm Brown's friend." "But you—surely you are the famous Mr. Jones?" "No, sir; I am Robinson. Jones's friend."

A friend of mine tells me that when, years ago, he began to learn the violin in a tailor's dingy little shop up a back yard, at the rate of one shilling per hour, a conductor of a local band for concerts wanted him to join. He replied that he could not play properly yet; to which the jolly conducducter answered, "Do you know the *notes* ?" My friend said he thought he did, but that he was not at all sure as to the harmonics. "Oh, you'll do for us, no doubt," added the enthusiastic and encouraging head of local music. "Why, bless your life, the little squeaks you make will not be heard amongst the tremendous fanfare of trumpets, harps, sackbuts, psalteries, dulcimers, and all kinds of music." (?) It is a fact, of course, that a noise may be disguised by an accompaniment, so long as the latter be only loud enough. There is nothing like the noise of London cabs rattling over the streets to shut out other unwelcome noises. Again, there is nothing like distance to improve the sound of bagpipes. One could, hearing them from afar, fancy they were bells. Distance disguises sounds almost as much as a loud accompaniment. The fact is that in the one case the irregularity in the order of vibrations, is less distinctly appreciated at a distance, and in the other, that the irregularity of the vibrations produced by one series of sounds is made less manifest by that of others, and perhaps even a kind of average is produced which is more or less regular. If this is so, the fact that when one listens at some distance to the sounds emanating from a church or chapel, during the singing of a hymn in many different keys and according to many different degrees of pitch, one is not greatly struck by the want of harmony, is explicable. In this and similar cases distance lends enchantment to the song.

With regard to playing in large orchestras, it may be said that it is much easier to play under these circumstances than it is to play a solo. Amateurs are often very nervous when playing a violin solo, and they have perhaps more reason to be so than than have solo-singers.

5. Another point with regard to holding the violin worthy of notice, is the placing of the left elbow and arm well under the violin. Some teachers neglect to lay the great stress which it is absolutely necessary to lay in this matter. They insist more strongly on the details which are of necessity involved in placing the elbow and fore-arm well under the instrument. Now, if the elbow be placed so as to be well under the violin, and near to the chest, but not in contact with it, the correct position of the fingers, and their readiness to fall upon the strings properly, will follow without the least difficulty. When the pupil pays strict and careful attention to the first point mentioned, he will find it not an arduous task to master the concomitant details; but when he neglects, by forgetfulness or carelessness, to keep his fore-arm and elbow well under the fiddle and near the chest, the utmost reiteration of the necessity of observing the consequent points is entirely lost upon him. If the beginner

SOME RULES TO BE OBSERVED IN PLAYING.

endeavours to keep the elbow and fore-arm well under the instrument, it will be found in the same proportion easy to keep the fingers in the right position on the strings, to hold the violin properly, and to make the shifts with comparative freedom; but when the first and fundamental point is neglected, it is utterly useless attempting to observe the others. The keeping of the elbow and fore-arm well under the violin is at first difficult, irksome, and painful in the extreme. It is an arduous task with some people, even for a year or more, and it is very easy to forget altogether the necessity for doing it. Constant attention and watching on the part of both pupil and teacher are needed. When this most important rule is not observed, violin-playing is very unsatisfactory both to the player and the hearers. One consequence of failing to carry out this rule is that the use of the fourth finger is rendered extremely difficult, especially when one is playing rapid passages on the G-string

6. The neck of the violin must not rest in the hollow between the thumb and fore-finger? With regard to the thumb, it should not press forcibly and rigidly against the neck; but the neck should be held lightly, and at the same time firmly, and simply rest, so that the shifts can be easily made, between the thumb and the third groove or crease of the fore-finger, so that there is a space between the neck and the hollow formed by the thumb and fore-finger sufficiently large to admit of a finger being passed through.

Should the fiddle be held so that its neck lies in the hollow of the thumb, the fingers other than the little one would extend too high above the finger-board, while the little finger, on the contrary, could only be made to approach the finger-board with pain, and again, the loose flesh in the hollow between finger and thumb would cling to the neck of the violin, and impede the shifting power of the hand. Much practice is required before the violin can be held properly, *i.e.*, firmly, but not rigidly.

7. The extreme tips of the fingers should be used for stopping the strings, and the correct position of the lower joints of the fingers when used for stopping should be carefully noted.

The terminal joints of the fingers should be exactly at right angles with the long axis of the finger-board. Care must be taken to hold the hand well over and round the finger-board, so that all four fingers can be readily used for stopping.

8. The proper situation of the fingers in relation to the finger-board involves a kind of doubling up of the joints of the first finger. If this rule is not observed, the other fingers will not come properly forward as they ought to do, so as to lie in a line parallel to that of the strings.

9. Take care that the fourth finger never gets underneath the finger-board. There is always a decided tendency for it to slip down, on account of its weakness, and this tendency must be constantly watched and checked.

Especial care must be taken to prevent this, when placing the third finger down upon the strings. At first it will be well to let the fourth finger rise up straight, when the third finger is being used. As time goes on, the learner will gain the power of bending the fourth finger almost as easily as the others. The fourth finger must be carefully watched, while one is stopping with the third. If it goes under the finger-board, leave off, and begin again. The practice of an exercise for this purpose, in which the fourth finger has to be very often used immediately after the third, would be found highly advantageous to the pupil. The tutor should provide the pupil with such an one. The imperfection of the fourth finger is a great difficulty both in pianoforte and in violin-playing.

10. Take care that you stop the strings with your fingers, before passing the bow over them, or at any rate exactly at the time of moving the bow. It is not an uncommon fault among beginners to pass the bow over, before stopping the string, and hence the note of the open string, or that of the stopped string, as the case may be, is produced as well as that of the string stopped as intended.

Again, never take a finger from the strings, unless obliged to do so; because, if the same note recur, as it

SOME RULES TO BE OBSERVED IN PLAYING.

may, the correct position, if the finger is allowed to remain in its place, is thereby already secured. Moreover, the taking up of the fingers unnecessarily tends to disturb the position of the hand and of the fingers.

Again, never take up a finger from a string, until you have finished playing that note, and have stopped the note that is to follow. If this rule is neglected, you may have an additional sound, from the string first stopped being let loose before the bowing on it is finished. The sound of the open string will be produced, and of course spoil the piece.

11. It is to be borne in mind that the tips of the fingers must be kept fixedly in contact with the correct point of the string. They must not be allowed to deviate. A difference of a very small fraction of a note is distinctly appreciable. Again, the pressure of the fingers upon any given string or strings must exceed that of the bow, since otherwise a poor and uncertain tone will be developed. If this necessity is not observed, the vibrations caused by the bow, which ought to stop at the point touched by the fingers, will extend beyond, and then the *tone* is spoiled entirely. The tips of the fingers should also in every case be brought firmly down upon the strings and preserve their pressure, since without this firmness, a good round tone is impossible, whether the playing be *piano* or *forte*.

12. In all cases the finger-nails should be pared rather closely, since otherwise they are liable to cut the string, and interfere with what is so necessary in violin-playing, a clear and firm contact between the fleshy tip of the finger and the string. Some difficulty may be experienced at first, by reason of the effect of the pressure of the fingers on the strings. The beginner need not be disheartened on this account. All violinists have had this obstacle to contend with and overcome. After some little time a horny epidermal growth takes place on the finger-tips, which obviates all pain, and also provides for the more effectual stopping of the strings.

13. Here we would call attention to a very useful diagram by Mr. Frederick W. Chanot, of Wardour Street, London, marking the positions of the fingers for the production of the different notes. We strongly recommend our readers to study it, as they will be thereby aided in finding the correct places for the notes with accuracy. At the same time we cannot advise that the original should be pasted on the finger-board, since doing so tends to make the learner trust to, and rely upon unnecessary help, instead of trying to cultivate the ear and the faculty of judging distance rightly. In fact, when the violin is held up to the chin, it is very difficult to see these marks. Moreover, the eye of the pupil should be fixed on his music, and not on the finger-board. In short, it may be said that most contrivances which are used for the purpose of saving trouble very often in the end serve but to increase the learner's difficulties. A thin strip of paper, however, just at the point where the third position begins on the finger-board, may be useful for a time. It should not be employed too long; but should be dispensed with, as soon as the learner is able to manage without it.

14. Notice especially the correct position of the first finger, in order to stop the first F natural which occurs on the E-string. The fault with most beginners is that they here produce F sharp, instead of F natural. The first finger must be placed much nearer to the nut, in stopping this F natural, than is necessary in producing, the first A natural which occurs on the G-string, the first E natural on the D-string, or the first B natural on the A-string.

With regard to the judging of distance on the violin, the following anecdote may amuse. A tenant-farmer, being present at a concert with his daughter, and observing the players busily at work with their violins and violoncellos, made the following remark:—"Well, my lass, I don't think I could learn to fiddle on the little fiddles, but I think I could manage to play one of them big fiddles, seeing as how they don't seem to be particular to an inch or two on them."

SOME RULES TO BE OBSERVED IN PLAYING.

Special attention should be paid, not only to the marks common to all music, such as crescendo, staccato, etc., but also to those which especially relate to the violin; for instance, the mark which indicates a down-bow, and the mark which means an up-bow. The French words used are very expressive. They are "tirez" and "poussez," of which the former denotes "pull the bow" and represents a down-stroke, while the latter means "push the bow" and represents an up-stroke. The terms "up" and "down" are likely to mislead the pupil. For instance, that which is called an up-bow on the G-string seems in reality to be a down-bow, and *vice versa*.

15. The player must be perfectly self-possessed, and allow nothing to disconcert or confuse him. The least nervous excitement or hurry is ruinous to good playing. In fact, the mind of the player should be bent on one thing, and on one thing only. There should be a fixed purpose and earnest determination to play the piece as well as it can possibly be played. Neither the audience nor the personality of the performer should be thought of, but only the work itself.

An acquaintance used to succeed remarkably well on the violin, when playing in the seclusion of his own chamber, to a few friends; but, when the occasion was more important, by reason of the presence of many, he failed lamentably. After playing a few bars, and not satisfying himself he would exclaim during his performance, "I hope you're not getting tired. I shall soon get through the piece." The effect on his playing may be imagined. It is true that lack of confidence is often a sign of deficiency, but there is no doubt that in some cases it is rather the result of a kind of natural self-depreciation, arising probably from the very high ideal in one's mind.

16. It is difficult to practice p.p. notes on the violin, especially when they have to be long drawn out. The beginner must guard against a tendency (*a*) to produce no tone at all; (*b*) to produce intermittent sounds; (*c*) to give the bow a tremulous or swaying motion. This is still more

difficult when double-stopping p.p. Let the beginner draw the bow steadily and firmly, and refrain from jerking it.

17. With regard to judging distance, some persons judge wrongly, and in order to correct their mistake, glide up or down to the correct distance for the pitch required. One often observes this method being used by fairly good players. The best safeguard against such a habit is to have private practice, and to play the given note again and again, until one can find it accurately.

18. In playing triplets, be careful to practice each note evenly. Many players treat a triplet, as though it were composed of one long note and two as short again, *e.g.*, as a crochet and two quavers, or a quaver and two semi-quavers.

19. In playing several bars of semi-quavers, there is a tendency which must be checked, to play them as follows, *e.g.*, the bar No. 1 is played as No. 2.

20. When playing, remember always the words of Sir Philip Sydney " Who will adhere to him that abandons himself ?" and also, that " courage mounteth with occasion " (Shakespeare). No person who suffers from intense nervousness ought to attempt singing or playing in public. At the same time, we do not regard the malady as incurable. In order to combat this very serious obstacle, we would recommend the cultivation of perseverance, self-confidence, and determination, coupled, of course, with as thorough a mastery over the work in hand as is possible.

CHAPTER X.

DOUBLE-STOPS, HARMONICS, SHIFTS, AND THE SHAKE.

A. DOUBLE-STOPPING.

DOUBLE-STOPPING is manifestly more difficult than single-stopping, because two notes, instead of one, must be in perfect tune. If either is out of tune, so also, of course, is the interval. Double-treble and quadruple-stopping occur in violin-playing. The term "double-stopping," however, may be used generically for all—double, treble, or quadruple. One fault frequently made by many beginners in playing a chord is that they play the notes of which it is composed successively, instead of simultaneously. Some double-stops are very difficult to play, inasmuch as they involve a very awkward position of the fingers. In some cases, great care must be taken, when playing a chord, not to allow the fingers which are stopping certain strings to touch contiguous strings. For instance, in playing a chord in which the A and the G-strings are stopped and the D-string is left open, the beginner must beware of touching the latter. In playing this chord, and similar ones, it is necessary to use the greatest care, in order to avoid touching the open string which intervenes. It is much to be regretted that there are not to be found in exercise-books good exercises for all the double-stops. The beginner should ask his teacher to write out a large number of exercises for double-stops, and these should be practised assiduously, so that, when met with in a piece, they can be readily stopped at once. The beginner should not be content, until he can play each interval and each chord in perfect tune and with perfect ease; for we must remember that, when playing a piece, there is no time admissible for trying to find the exact spots for the notes. The fingers should be in readiness at once to drop upon the precise spots. As a rule, too, many players bow the double and triple-stops much more feebly than they do the rest of the passages in a piece. Too frequently, also, amateurs break the chord, by half lifting the bow over each string. These habits should be most carefully avoided. When a triple or quadruple-stop is to last some time, as it is impossible to devote the whole of the time to all the notes of the chord, the last two strings should be dwelt upon. The necessity of this is owing to the curve of the bridge; for, if the bridge were quite flat, then a chord might be played just as it is upon the piano, *i.e.* all the notes of the chord might be dwelt upon, for any given length of time. The learner should be very careful and assiduous in his practice of double-stopping.

B. Harmonics.

When harmonics are to be played, a small mark like O or ◇ is placed above the note. The method of placing the finger so as to produce harmonics is to touch the string in the ordinary way at the given point, but to fix it very gently and lightly, with the tip of the finger resting easily upon the string. There must be actual contact between the tip of the finger and the string, and yet the string is not to be pressed down, nor must it be pressed at all. The slighter the touch, the better is the sound produced. The bowing is the same as for ordinary simple notes. There is a peculiar flute-like tone, which is characteristic of the so-called harmonics.

Harmonics are used for effect. Some of the highest of them are produced by means of the lowest part of the G-string, and the same harmonics can be formed by acting upon different parts of other strings.

It will be a great help to the beginner to remember that all the *harmonics*, *i.e.* parts of the strings where the harmonics are to be produced lie *parallel* to one another.

Attention should be given to the instruction-book for the violin of Berthold Tours, as he devotes a whole chapter to the detailed consideration of harmonics. His description is very clear, and the pupil will do well to study the chapter with great care. For the theory of harmonics, the reader is referred to the work entitled "Sensations of Tone," by Hermann L. F. Helmholtz, M.D., translated by Alexander J. Ellis, or to Professor Tyndall's work on "Sound."

It is, however, just as well perhaps to caution the reader with regard to the use of the word "*harmonic*." This term has been employed to designate both the compound tones, such as those above mentioned, and also the simple upper partial tones, of which any given compound tone is really composed. Simple upper partial tones, that is, the partial tones of any given note, exclusive of the prime tone (which is generally loudest and determines the pitch), even when *harmonic*, must be distinguished from the sounds called "*harmonics*," which can be produced on a violin or harp, for instance. Such "harmonics" are not necessarily *simple* tones, but are more generally compounds of some of the *partial tones*, which combine to produce the musical tone of the whole string. These partial tones which give rise to the so-called "harmonic" are selected by damping the remainder, as can be done in the case of the violin, by the method above referred to. When one listens to the gradual cessation of the sound produced by a pianoforte-string, which has been struck and not damped, one hears the fading harmonics. These also are compound, and not simple partial tones.

C. Remarks on the Shift.

The first, second, third, fourth, fifth, and sixth positions can only be well learnt from a good violinist. The second position is sometimes called the *half-shift*, and the third position the *whole shift*. The term "shift" derives its name from the shifting of the first finger, so as, for instance, to play G instead of F on the E-string with the first finger. This is the half-shift, or second position. The whole shift, or third position, consists in placing the fingers, for instance, in such a manner that the first finger touches the point for

F

producing the note A on the E-string. A very good practice for the shift is to be obtained by playing an exercise arranged for one position in that one position, and keeping to that position on all the strings. One precaution with regard to shifts should be observed. The beginner should never lose his hold of the place where the first finger rests, unless it is absolutely necessary. Indeed, in all cases, as mentioned above, the rule should be observed that no finger should be taken off the strings unless it is quite unavoidable. It often happens that a particular note has to be played frequently. If, then, the finger is placed so as to ensure that note, the player will not be obliged to find it again. Besides this, the correct position of the hand will be kept with more ease, if this rule is observed.

The following advice with regard to the shift is taken from an eminent violinist, though the words are slightly altered here and there:—

"Take a violin part and play it upon the half-shift, *i.e.*, with the first-finger upon G on the first string, and constantly keep upon this shift, playing the whole piece without moving the hand from this position, unless A on the fourth string be wanted, or D upon the first. In that case you should afterwards return again to the half-shift, without ever moving the hand down to the natural position. This practice should be continued until you can execute at sight and with facility upon the half-shift any violin part not intended as a solo. After this, advance the hand on the finger-board to the whole shift, with the first finger upon A on the first string, and learn to play any part with ease upon this shift. When certain of this, advance to the double shift, with the first finger upon B on the first string. When sure of that likewise, pass to the fourth position of the hand, making C with the finger upon the first string."

To the beginner, it is always an extremely difficult matter to judge relative distance accurately enough to be able to play well with the hand in the various different positions. The half-shift, or second position, is generally found to be the most troublesome; and especially is the playing of

DOUBLE-STOPS, HARMONICS, SHIFTS, THE SHAKE.

rapid passages an arduous task, since a quick change of position is then necessitated. The pupil should observe carefully the numbers used to designate the various shifts. The word itself is not marked, but a number placed over any given note shows how it is to be played. For instance, if the first note A which is produced on the E-string is to be played on the whole shift—that is, with the hand in the third position—the number 1 will be placed over it. This indicates that the note A in question is to be played by stopping with the first finger, instead of with the third. One must mark also the change of numbers, whereby one is directed to descend to the first or ordinary position again. Moreover, when changing from one position to another, it is very necessary to avoid pulling the violin from under the chin, or allowing it to swerve aside. In this connection it is obvious that the instrument should be held with sufficient firmness, in order that it may not slip out of the grasp of the player.

D. THE SHAKE.

It is a very difficult matter to produce a good shake. The following is taken from Tartini :—

"The shake should be practised slowly, moderately fast, and quickly; for in practice the same shake will not serve with equal propriety for a slow movement, as for a quick one. The learner should commence with an open string, sustain the note with a swell, and begin the shake very slowly, increasing in quickness by insensible degrees, until the shake becomes a rapid one. There must be no skip, but a gradation between a semiquaver and a demi-semi-quaver. There should be an increase in velocity, when one is practising the shake, in the same degree as there is in loudness in making a swell. The shake should be practised with all the fingers in turn."

In the performance of the shake, the rule as to bringing the fingers very firmly down on the strings must be most carefully observed; since otherwise a very feeble and indefinte shake is the result.

HOW TO PLAY THE FIDDLE.

Another great point to be observed in the production of a good shake is that it should, whether quick or slow, be quite even, both in regard to time, and also in regard to equal pressure of the finger used. Some players begin a shake well, but spoil it towards the end, and make an uneven and intermittent shake, through inattention to these matters. Again, many beginners do not take the trouble to ascertain whether the shake in question should be one of two whole notes or of two semitones. The turn which usually follows the shake should be well considered, and should not be produced with an abrupt jerk, but smoothly and evenly. The necessity of having the fingers well on the finger-board, and that of not allowing the finger to slip underneath, must always be remembered.

As we said above, the shake should be practised with all the fingers. Begin with the first and second, then practise with the second and third, and lastly with the third and fourth. It is important not to make an unnecessary change in the position of the hand, in order to shake always with the first or second fingers. It may be added that nothing tends to increase the strength and flexibility of the third and fourth fingers so much as constant practice of the shake with them.

CHAPTER XI.

PLAYING WITH AN ACCOMPANIMENT.

"What! when I had played three bars thus, you could not guess that I should hurry the fourth, and droop with a melodious sigh upon the fifth! You dare to strike in at the end of a note which my intention would have stretched out into at least another semibreve! You are untrue to the ryhthm of my soul. You want to take the initiative; you must always be creating; you think you know best; you impose your reading upon me. What! you will do this when I am the soloist or the singer!" (Haweis, in "My Musical Life," vol. i, p. 64).

ALTHOUGH playing with a piano accompaniment is very common among violinists, we do not recommend it where an accompaniment from a second violin, a violoncello, or harp, is at hand. With regard to playing with an accompaniment, as indeed also in reference to all musical performances, there are three chief points which must be considered separately. All the three considerations, tone, tune, and time, are to be regarded in connection with playing with an accompaniment. Excellence, or want of it, is in such a case more markedly conspicuous than in solo-playing, because either or both of the two performers may be in fault. It must be always borne in mind that, to do full justice to the conditions required for the production of good tone, tune, and time, far more skill is required in violin-playing than in playing on the piano. It has already been mentioned in another chapter that while the timbre of a piano depends entirely on the talent of the maker, that of a violin is not to the same extent determinately fixed. It can be affected in some slight degree by the power of the player. It may even be allowed in the case of pianos that an accomplished pianist can play so as to modify the sound emanating from the instrument by the differences in his touch of the various keys, in such a manner that the tone of a bad piano will not strike so painfully upon the ear. Pianos vary considerably in tone, as every one knows—so much so, in fact, that a connoisseur can in many cases tell the maker's name by hearing an instrument played. There are very many conditions which must be observed, and many small details which must be attended to in the making of pianos. For instance, the hammers are covered in all cases with a soft and yielding material, in order to produce a full rich tone. This is necessary; but it is also essential that the exact spot where the hammer should fall be determined, since the number of upper partials, *i.e.*, the quality of tone, depends to a very great extent on this point being correctly fixed. (*) The tone of a violin, on the other hand, is not so accurately defined in the same sense as is that of a piano. Of course, the violins of the old masters, 'Stradivari, Guarneri, Amati, and so on, are always acknowledged to possess a power of producing good tone in a high degree, and, being far superior to those of other makers, are sold at much higher prices. At the same time, a good violinist can produce a far better tone by means of an inferior violin, than an inexperienced player can from a good one. Many an amateur can draw no better tone out of a genuine violin by Stradivari, than he can out of an ordinary fiddle. Indeed, in order that beauty of tone may be heard, a fine instrument and a fine player are both essential.

One more remark with regard to tone may be made. In playing with an accompaniment, there should be no great incongruity between the tone of the violin and that of the instrument used for accompanying. Though, for many reasons, we can scarcely recommend beginners to play with a piano acompaniment, unless no other means of practising time-keeping and the securing of harmonious

---

(*) The force and character of the upper partial tones of a string which is vibrating depend on:—
  1. The nature of the stroke.
  2. The point struck.
  3. The density, rigidity, and elasticity of the string

PLAYING WITH AN ACCOMPANIMENT

co-existence in sounds is practicable, we may most certainly emphasise the statement that a good violin does not harmonise with a bad piano.

With regard to tone, both instruments should, if possible, possess similar characteristics. A piano should be used the tone of which as nearly as possible corresponds to that of the violin in question. One naturally objects to hear a violin of fine tone played together with a piano which has only a poor or bad timbre. In fact, without good timbre there can be no true music. Music depends quite as much on tone as on tune and time. Many an amateur may sing or play in as good *tune* and *time* as an Albani or a Joachim respectively; but very few musicians would care to listen to these amateurs at a concert, unless they produced a good tone. In singing, especially, the *timbre* or *tone* of the voice is the charm which induces persons to pay large prices for a seat at a concert, and incites the great singers to ask so much for their performances. No one who understood anything of music would be so foolish as to say that, if time and tune were accurate, the ear would not be pained by want of tone. Tone or timbre, is, in short, a most important element in music; and it is to this that the thrilling fascination of good music is in great part due.

In the next place, with regard to tune, the difference between the violin and the piano is still more decided. While in the piano the tune, both absolute and relative, is fixed decidedly by the piano-tuner, that of the violin depends solely upon the violinist. All that is required of the pianoforte-player with regard to tune is to know which are the keys corresponding to the notes required to be produced, and to strike or press them in the right manner. If the instrument is out of tune, it is not the player, but the tuner or the owner, who is considered to be responsible for the fault. No one would think of blaming a pianist for playing out of tune on a piano which in itself was not properly tuned; except, indeed, that the player ought perhaps, when it is possible, to refrain from further playing when it has been learnt that such is the case. It would not be expected, of course, that the player should be able to go through the process of tuning the instrument The requisite skill to do so would not be looked for in a pianist. Indeed, scarcely would the necessary accuracy of ear be supposed to be possessed by every pianist. The violinist, on the other hand is not only looked down upon, if he or she plays out of tune, but is also expected to be able to do these two things, viz. to play in tune on a violin not in perfect tune, and also to tune the instrument. Moreover, it is necessary to possess the power of tuning a violin during the performance of a concerted piece, while counting the bars in the meantime. Should one be the only primo, one must be able to judge distance so well as to make allowance for the slipping of the pegs, or slackening of the strings while playing. It is, in fact, reckoned a very poor excuse for a person playing out of tune to be able to say, " My violin is out of tune."

If the piano is not correctly tuned, and the violin is played in tune, the discord is not really the fault of either player, except in so far as the pianist ought to have ensured that the piano was in tune, and also inasmuch as both ought to stop playing at once, when it is practicable to do so. The piano ought to be perfectly tuned, and the violin ought also to be played in perfect tune. It very often happens that a violin with a pianoforte accompaniment sounds atrociously. When both players play well, this is to be accounted for by the fact that very few people will go to the small amount of expense and trouble necessary for keeping their pianos in good tune. Very many also do not have the best, or even good, pianos.

Thirdly, with regard to time, the difficulty of being precise in keeping time is markedly greater in the case of the fiddle than it is in that of a piano. The pianist has the bass cleff as a guide to the treble; and it is certainly far easier to play a crotchet with one hand while playing two quavers with the other, or a minim with one hand and two crotchets or four quavers with the other, or any other duly proportioned combinations, in perfect time, than it is to play anything written for one hand alone. Let a pianist play only the notes on the treble cleff of a piece. It will be found that the deeping of time is much more difficult than it is when playing the whole piece with the two hands. It is a well-known fact, too, that many who can play pieces on the piano in perfect time, and suppose themselves in consequence to be very good time-keepers, lose their confidence in this respect when they attempt to play correctly with regard to time upon the violin, even after they have learnt the instrument very fairly. Time is lost by many amateurs in passing the bow and fingers from one string to another, in changing from a down-bow to an up-bow, and *vice versa*, and in not being ready with the bow immediately after a rest.

Time-keeping seems to be the most general and the greatest difficulty experienced in playing with an accompaniment. There is generally fault on the part of both soloist and accompanist, and it is also generally extremely difficult to tell which player most deserves blame. It is, of course, very hard for the accompanist if the solo-violinist keeps really bad time; but it must be always remembered that the violinist must in this case be the leader, just as the singer should lead, when singing with an accompaniment. It is imperatively necessary that the accompaniment should follow the solo-part, and not be played independently of it. For this reason it is that the staff for the singer, and for solo performers in general, is placed above those of the accompaniment. If the soloist errs, the pianist should try to cover the mistake, and certainly not expose it. To accompany well is, in reality, a very difficult matter, especially for some players, and is certainly an art in itself, distinct to a great extent from that of playing well. It is not sufficient to be a good musician. Sympathetic passion, and what may be called intuitive foreknowledge are also requisite. These remarks apply in the case of all instruments used for accompanying; to pianos, harps, and so on. Some accompanists execute a solo on their own account, entirely forgetting the duty they have to perform. If there is to be an acceleration or relaxation in the time, they often judge of its degree for themselves, instead of allowing the soloist to rule in the matter. The consequence is, that it is only the most experienced soloists who can play at all with such as these, and even then it is a most unsatisfactory performance; inasmuch as the soloist and accompanist really change places, the soloist following the accompanist, the cart preceding the horse. A beginner should be very careful to play with a good accompanist. Indeed the best, and, in fact, the only test of good time-keeping in the case of a solo performance is to be found in this way. There are only two admissible modes of correction, when the soloist errs in time-keeping. One plan which is the only one that can be employed in public, is to cover the mistakes as well as possible. The mistakes may be referred to and, if necessary, may be commented on afterwards. The other method which is admissible only in private during a practice, is to stop short immediately when the error is made, and begin the bar again. In all casses, it is the duty of the soloist to count time, and not to rely upon the accompaniment or accompanist.

(1) We would here call the attention of the reader to a faulty practice too commonly indulged in. In order to facilitate time-keeping, many beginners divide a note, say three or four beats into separate parts, thus making several notes instead of one. Suppose, *e.g.*, that a bar consisting of a dotted crochet and three quavers, occurs in 6-8 time. In this case they divide the dotted crochet into three quavers.

The consequence is that the evenness of the *dotted crochet* is lost altogether, and a jerking motion is produced which is most unsatisfactory. The temptation to play in this way is still greater, when one *note* is tied through several bars, as *e.g.*, in the following bars.

PLAYING WITH AN ACCOMPANIMENT.

Let the beginner try to count mentally without imparting to his bow the beats of time which are going on in his mind, and which may also occur in the accompaniment.

(2) We would call attention to another difficulty which besets the beginner. Suppose he is playing a piece with several bars of crochets and quavers, and he then came to a few bars of semiquavers, very probably he will play the semiquavers only half as fast again as the quavers, or perhaps twice as fast as they should be played. He may, however, as a beginner does, do something worse than this, viz., run helter skelter through the bars of semiquavers, as rapidly as possible without any regard to time, omitting a few difficult notes here and there.

Again, when playing by one's self, it is necessary to count all the rests. One must not *imagine* that one has counted them, and pass them by, since, if this is done, it may happen that, when one is playing with an accompaniment, there may be an inability to know when to begin again. Count the rests always, unless beating time is preferred. After a little practice in audible counting, silent counting will be found to be the most convenient method, and quite as satisfactory as beating time with the foot.

A propos of rests and resting, the following anecdote is amusing. Old Jacob Astley once observed a fiddler in his band resting, while the others were playing, and thinking him idle, began to reprimand him for his apparent laziness. The violinist tried to explain to the irate old gentleman that there were several bars marked with a rest. "Rest!" exclaimed Astley; "don't tell me about rest, sir! I pay you to come here and play, sir, not to rest."

Time-keeping is a most essential requirement, and should be most carefully studied. It is recorded of Charles I., King of Spain, who was a violinist, that he played well, "with the trifling drawbacks of missing his notes, and breaking the time, as if to show his royal independence." Let not this be said of the beginner. It is important to avoid the habit of pulling the beat, and also that of dragging it. Some players, when excited, are apt to do the former, and, when dull or tired, to do the latter. Should this occur in a band, the conductor does not leave the players in the lurch, but alters his time to suit them. In such a case the players may be spoken of as having respectively either pulled or dragged the conductor's beat.

The phrasing of a passage must also be attended to, otherwise the whole piece falls flat. As a rule, the first beat of a bar should be marked and emphatic, the second decidedly less so, the third a little less marked than the first, and the fourth as much marked as the second. Beginners and amateurs, either as soloists or when playing in a band, have a tendency to commit a twofold error, viz., that of producing a "disproportionate acceleration of time in a quick and loud passage, and a disproportionate delay in a slow and *piano* movement." This habit can be overcome by the help of a skilful master.

The reading of music is also a point requiring much care. The player should develop a capacity for "reading onwards," as, unless the power of doing so is possessed awkward breaks in the music are apt to occur. With this power every reader of books is more or less acquainted. While playing a given bar, the eyes and mind should be partly fixed upon a few following bars.

Execution must also be considered. Some pieces and some passages require powerful execution; while others need much less. The power of playing with execution will only be gained after long practice. A piece should be learnt as thoroughly as possible, and then, when well known, the various marks and guides can be observed still more thoroughly in detail. It is well also for the amateur to seek advice as to the best manner of execution, in the case of a difficult piece, from a good professional violinist. It may happen that, when one is playing, a chord might be found to be out of tune. Should this arise from any reason—for example, the slipping of a peg—it should at once be detected, and the cause of the error rectified. Friends, who perhaps know nothing about the violin, and are in no sense to be accounted competent judges in regard to the manner in which a given piece should be played, are apt sometimes to make remarks about the taste with which a given piece is executed. It is wise not to be led away by such talk, whether it be praise or blame. When playing, forget that you have an audience, and concentrate your attention with firm determination on the best means of playing the piece thoroughly.

CHAPTER XII.

CONCLUDING REMARKS.

"Music is the only sensual gratification which mankind may indulge in to excess without injury to their moral or religious feelings."—ADDISON.

> "Be not afeard; the isle is full of noises,
> Sounds, and sweet airs, that give delight and hurt not.
> Sometimes a thousand twangling instruments
> Will hum about mine ears; and sometimes voices,
> That, if I then had wak'd after long sleep,
> Will make me sleep again."
> SHAKESPEARE.

ALL sounds are dependent upon the vibrations of particles of matter, whether it be solid, liquid, or gaseous. These vibrations are propagated to the ear by the medium of waves in the air. It is somewhat difficult to understand this thoroughly. One must think of the effect produced upon a surface of water by the fall of a stone upon it from a height. It is, perhaps, better to look at the waves of the sea, as they are tossed to and fro by the numerous forces which produce and act upon them. The case of waves of sound is, however, far more complex, and far more involved. The fact is, that we must look upon the waves as affecting spherical volumes of air. It is exceedingly difficult to realise this. The vibrations of each particle must not be confounded with the waves, by means of which the disturbance shown by vibration is propagated from spherical layer to spherical layer. Again, the vibration in the case of air results in the productions of layers of greater, and layers of less, density. The spherical layers are alternately condensed and rarefied.

The auditory nerves conduct the excitations or disturbances produced in them to the brain. The brain, in its turn, transforms the excitations or stimuli which it thus receives, into sensations of sound, more or less pleasurable as the case may be. Musical sounds differ from noises, in that they result from the conduction of waves of vibrations which are regularly periodic in character, to the ear. The waves of which noises are composed are irregular and disturbed. It is, of course, to a large extent a question of degree, inasmuch as it is often very difficult indeed to say whether any given sound or series of sounds most nearly approaches a noise or music. Authorities not unfrequently differ as to their decision. There are some who can find beautiful music in the rumbling and rippling of the waves on a sandy beach. There are some who can detect the musical value of the sound of carriage-wheels. There are some who can listen with pleasure for hours to the strange combination of sounds produced by a cataract or a waterfall. Nay, there are some who think that the highest function of music is to bring out clearly the unison between our thoughts and the sounds we hear around us in every part of nature. Some regard music as the language of our highest sentiments and feelings. "These motions, *i.e.* rhythms and melodies, are active, and action is the sign of feeling" (Aristotle).

It is almost impossible that any sound should be entirely composed of regularly recurring waves. On the contrary, probably in all cases, even the purest notes contain some

CONCLUDING REMARKS.

which are produced irregularly. The great difficulty is to make perfectly pure sounds which at the same time possess good tone. Indeed, a musical instrument may be said to be a machine by means of which we can produce at will those regular waves of the air, which are needed to make musical sounds.

The characters of a musical sound may be considered under the following three heads:—

1. Tone, quality, or timbre, which depends on the form of the vibrations.

2. Intensity or loudness which is determined by the amplitude of the vibrations.

3. Pitch, which is determined by the number of vibrations in a given time.

Let us consider each of these very briefly.

The tone of a musical instrument depends upon the number, order, and intensity of the vibrations of the "over-tones" or "upper partials," which characterise the different notes produced by it. It is very difficult to express, so as to explain in a few words fully and clearly, what is really meant by tone. Every musician, however, knows how to distinguish, practically, good from bad tone. The reader should refer to Helmholtz's "Sensations of Tone," in order to gain an intimate acquaintance with what is known concerning this intricate subject.

It is very seldom, and perhaps it may even be said to never be the case, that any given note is a single and simple one. White light is in reality composed of many different orders of vibrations, which give rise, when it is split up and decomposed, to the different colours of the rainbow and the spectrum. Similarly, nearly all musical sounds consist in reality of a large number of sounds. As a rule, each apparently simple sound is compound, being composed of numerous other notes less markedly, but none the less really, produced. These determine the quality or tone of the note. (It is unfortunate that the word "tone" is sometimes also used as a synonym for the term "note.") The difference in quality between sounds of the same pitch chiefly depends, then, upon the number and intensity of the constituent sounds of which they are composed. The lowest constituent of a musical sound is that which determines its pitch. The "upper partials" are not separately and individually heard; but they serve the purpose of enriching the fine notes of good instruments and of good singers. The form of the vibrations, and therefore that of the waves, of which a sound may be said to be composed, determines the tone. The form of the waves of necessity results from the influence of all the constituent waves. Of course, the noise of the machinery by which notes are produced, the striking, the jars, and so on, also affect the tone. Generally speaking, however, the noise of the machinery is scarcely included in the word "tone." In the case of a fairly good instrument being played by a good musician, the incidental noise produced would not be great. Mellowness or roundness of tone, as opposed to harshness, is the chief distinguishing characteristic between the old and the newly made violins; and this fine quality of tone is displayed, whether the playing and execution be powerful or otherwise. The volume of air enclosed in a violin-box corresponds to certain proper tones which it reinforces. The proper tone of the enclosed air may be found by blowing across one of the ƒ-holes, and has been investigated by Savart and others. A fine violin of the grand pattern by Stradivari, in the possession of Mr. Huggins, is said to have given a chief maximum resonance with from 260 to 268 vibrations per second, and a secondary but weaker maximum resonance with a note of about 252 vibrations per second. Mr. Ellis found, in the case of this same violin, and in that of one by Pietro Guarnerius, that every fork of his series was to some extent reinforced. This power of strengthening all the notes of the octave is of great importance, and depends upon very subtle conditions of the general form of the violin. It is also connected with the shape of the sound-holes, by the medium of which the air in the violin-box communicates with the external air. In

CONCLUDING REMARKS.

accordance also with the number of longitudinal fibres of the belly which are removed to form the sound-holes, the mode of vibration of the belly itself is greatly modified. The marked difference between the tone of different violins is somewhat difficult to explain, and requires much research; but it is well to know what is meant by the term "tone."

When we say that the tone of a Stainer violin, *e.g.*, is pure and silvery, and has a certain piercing quality, we really mean that the notes emitted from it are very strong in "upper partials." It has not the roundness of a violin by Guarnerius, because the "lower harmonics" are not so markedly present; nor has it the sweetness of one by Amati, because the upper partials are too strongly pronounced; nor, again has it the even breadth and power of a fiddle by Stradivari, because the harmonics produced with most of the notes are not so nicely graduated.

With regard to the intensity or loudness of musical sounds, it may be said that the amplitude of the vibrations is a measure of the loudness of a sound. As, however, can be easily seen by the aid of diagrams, the amplitude of the vibrations does not in any way affect their form and shape, and thus it follows that the loudness or power of a note does not interfere in the least with its mellowness. Nevertheless, some suppose that with a violin posessing a fine mellow tone, they will not be able to produce such powerful sounds as they could extract from a harsh or hard-toned instrument. The fact of the case, on the contrary, is that the utmost power can always go hand in hand with the utmost mellowness or richness of tone.

With reference to the other very important quality of a musical sound, the pitch, it may be said, that as the form of the waves of sound represents tone or timbre, and as the amplitude or width of the vibrations represents power, so the time of the vibrations determines the pitch of the note. This has been proved experimentally by the use of Savart's toothed wheel, and by the instrument commonly known as the "syren."

HOW TO PLAY THE FIDDLE.

Tone, loudness, and pitch are, then, independent of one another. Still, a note sung or played with bad tone is frequently spoken of as being out of tune. The fact of the case is, that a note of bad or poor timbre may be perfectly correct with regard to tune, that is, of true pitch; though at the same time it may be to some extent rightly spoken of as being "unmusical," or not produced in good tone. A violin of bad tone, or one played harshly, strikes the ears of listeners as sounding "not tuneful." A note may be sung or played correctly in point of pitch, and yet not be "tuneful" or "musical," *i.e.* it may be "in bad tone." The instrument, or the player, or the singer, may be at fault with regard to tone.

It is well to mention one more point. Some players have a decided taste for classical music, while others care for none but the more superficial. Without the least desire to disparage unduly the desire for the lighter kind, it may be said that it would be well if all would cultivate an appreciation of that which is deep and classical. Such appreciation depends on the character of the mind and on its training. Some are endowed naturally with a capacity for deep thought, and delight in deep matters generally; while others are only capable of understanding things which are very easy and light. There are some who would be inexpressibly bored by listening to a concert made up entirely of classical music. Bach's fugues irritate some people, and Beethoven's sonatas fall flat on the ears of a large number. Deep discourses are voted dry and uninteresting, simply because none but the highly educated, and those who are naturally well endowed, have the power to grasp them. At the same time, it must be borne in mind that the feeling of dislike for what is deep and thorough, is the more permanent the more it takes the form of blind unthinking prejudice. It is a curious fact that some object to any music that is called classical, while they really do not clearly comprehend what is meant and implied by the term. When a rooted prejudice has not taken hold of the mind, a taste for the grander and finer musical conceptions may be developed to a large

CONCLUDING REMARKS.

extent. Granting that this is the case, let the beginner on the violin be urged to cultivate a taste for what is really good and great in music. There is, however, in many forms of music that are not strictly classical, a tendency to cheer and relieve the human mind. Let us not hurriedly draw a distinct line of demarcation between the two tastes. There are many classical minds which can enjoy on occasion the more superficial forms of composition. In any case the student should be recommended to avoid what is *trashy*. Much music that is in the present day, composed and sent out to the world, is nothing more nor less than bad. When, however, we consider that there are very many songs and pieces, certainly superficial, which have obtained a hold on men's minds, and that although the greater number are almost worthless, some of them, nevertheless, are calculated to raise the whole tone of men's mental and moral nature, and to cheer the weary heart, we cannot condemn them altogether on the score of their triviality. All that we beg for, is that the musical student shall not shrink from the difficulties of good music. In spite of all that can be said, it is not every one who can hope to be deeply classical in taste. Some could never understand the deeper forms of music. The beginner should commence with the simpler forms of good music, and we can venture to say that, as time goes on, a more pure taste will be developed. The whole art of music is one which requires the utmost attention, and, in fact, a lifetime is almost too short for the true knowledge of the subtle intricacies of harmony and melody which man has been enabled to gather from the soulful systems of vibrations in all nature heard. We have now at length completed our "Hints to Beginners on the Violin." By Beginners we do not mean only those who are just starting, but all those who wish to mount higher and still ever higher on the road which leads to excellence, all those who may be looked upon as aspirants and beginners in the ever-radiant Temple of Fame and Glory!

Let us by way of conclusion quote from a writer on the violin the following advice in rhyme:—

HOW TO PLAY THE FIDDLE.

"FRIENDLY ADVICE TO THE YOUNG AMATEUR."
"First, let a rearward attic of your labours be the scene;
For such seclusion best for you (and others) is I ween.
In comfort then assume a chair, and be therein at ease.
Your fiddle in your left hand, and in your right the bow,
Learn, first, the dotted page, awhile, before *to work* you go.
Firm as a forceps be your wrist, but flexile as an eel!
And for that struggling shoulder-joint—just teach it to *be still;*
For, mark! the motion of the arm must be 'twixt wrist and elbow
Or else, howe'er you moil and toil, be sure you ne'er will well bow!
To guide each movement of the bow, to give it vital spring,
To send it bounding on its way—the wrist, the wrist's the thing!
Your bow's relation to the *strings* must keep a just right angle,
Or harshly else, and out of tune, your tortured notes will jangle.
From *heel* to point that bow now draw, with action slow and steady;
Then back again, and so repeat, till in such practice ready.
The same in quicker time then try, and next proceed to draw;
From *middle* (with a shorter scope) to *point* and back, see-saw.
This, too, in swifter time rehearse; and then like justice deal
Unto the other half of bow, from *middle* to the *heel.*
There is a word too seldom heard, *not* dear to young ambition,
But wholesome in its discipline—that word is "*repetition.*"
Content to glimmer ere you shine, leap not beyond your bounds!
From small beginnings rise great ends—'tis *pence* that make up *pounds*
From exercise to exercise, progressive through your book,
Work on—scales, intervals, and all, how dry soe'er they look!
Nor jerk forth scraps, or odds and ends, of every tune that floats.
Can any foolery be worse than scatt'ring of *loose notes?*
Let not thy steps untutored move! A master's ready skill,
For safety and for succour see, to curb or point thy will!
Plain work precedes all *ornament;* keep graces for a late
Achievement, since you first must *build* ere you can *decorate.*
Think elegance a pretty thing, but *breadth* a vast deal better;
Nor for sake of lesser charms, your larger movements fetter.
It is the pride of players great, a free and dashing bow,
As borne along on waves of sound to their success they go!
Corelli old contemn thou not! substantial, good, and plain,
He's like a round of British beef; he's "cut and come again"
In fiddle-practice, as in life, are difficulties gifts?
Yes, double stops are just the things to drive thee to thy shifts,
Bating no jot of heart or hope, toil, till in time's process,
The music that is in thy soul thy fiddle shall express."
            Altered slightly from GEORGE DUBOURG.

APPENDIX.

——o——

Our readers will understand that, although we have made some appreciable and important improvements in this revised and corrected edition, both by way of addition and also by way of alteration, still we have scarcely had time to render our little work as thoroughly complete as we desired to make it. In putting the pages through the press, it happened to be in this case a matter of very serious consideration that there should be no avoidable delay whatsoever. We had strong reasons for believing that orders for copies were continually coming in to the various booksellers, only to be received by the necessary but very ominous reply *out of print*. Hence we felt there was no time to lose; and indeed, so far as possible, we felt it incumbent upon us to send back the proofs by return of post. Thus it happens that these few hints which follow are not mentioned in their right place in the body of the work, and we have therefore thought well to add them here.

(1). When about to play with an accompaniment, be very careful to ensure that you begin to play precisely and exactly at the correct moment. If you are either too early or too late, much embarrassment and confusion will probably ensue, and it may be a matter of great anxiety to put things right. Indeed it is perhaps best to start afresh, and begin the piece again. It is most necessary, of course, that you should be playing those particular notes which are required of you at the same identical point of time as that at which your accompanist is executing the particular notes required of him or her. If you are a fraction too late or too early, the harmony is destroyed, and discord is the

APPENDIX.

inevitable result. If either you, the violinist on the one hand, or your accompanist on the other be ahead, even for a short time, it sounds very badly, and, excruciating torture is not too strong a word for the effect produced on sensitive ears, if this is kept up throughout the whole piece. In order to bring about the strictest accuracy in this respect, always make a point of counting aloud, before starting, a whole bar preceding the point of commencement

(2). It is very important indeed that all directions in regard to the velocity of a musical movement such as are expressed by such words as presto, allegro, allegretto, andante, adagio, and so on, should be carefully and implicitly observed. Otherwise the piece will be badly rendered, or perhaps even entirely spoiled. When learning allegros and especially prestos, it is well at first to practise them slowly, in order to gain a thorough mastery over them. As they become well known, the time can be greatly increased by degrees. This should be borne in mind, more particularly when a piece contains some passages which are at once difficult, and at the same time require to be rapidly performed. If this point is not attended to, *i.e.*, if these difficult quick movements have not been well learned, it will be necessary, in order to play them accurately, that they be played more slowly in proportion to the other parts than is correct. Thereby the phrasing of the piece as a whole will be destroyed.

(3). A metronome is useful; but its employment should be delayed, until the difficulties of a piece have been fairly overcome. Beethoven said on one occasion: " Let us have no metronome, for he who has a good ear does not need it, and to him who has not a good ear, it will be of no use." However, the great tone-poet spoke these words under circumstances of irritation, and they should therefore be taken *cum grano salis*. A judicious use of the metronome cannot fail to be of service, especially in the practice of exercises.

(4). In changing the time, be careful that both you on your side as the violinist, and on the other hand your companion the accompanist, are agreed upon the degree of acceleration

APPENDIX.

or diminution of the time which is to be observed. If this is not attended to, great confusion generally prevails.

(5). We would recommend the practice of beginning at a certain *beat* in a bar, instead of the habit of starting at the first beat always. This is a somewhat difficult acquisition for beginners; but it serves as a very useful lesson, since it tends to make the student more familiar with correct time-keeping.

(6). For purposes of study we would recommend the following music :—

(*a*). Pleyel's Duetts for two violins, Op. 8, Op. 48, and Op. 59. The two former may be obtained as arranged for a piano accompaniment.

(*b*). Maza's Duetts for two violins. Op. 38; Cah. I. and II. Op. 39: Cah. I. and II., Op. 40: Cah. I. and II., Op. 41: Cah. I. and II.

(*c*). Beethoven's Sonatas as arranged for violin and piano. These works of perhaps the greatest composer of music who has ever lived, are certainly very difficult to learn. They are, however, to be considered as perfect masterpieces of extreme beauty, and they possess a deep and subtle power which surpasses all description. They are labours of care and love, and shew a sustained and enduring pathos most thrilling and even weird in its calm and solemn grandeur. It is not too much to say that these are unique productions of sublime genius, piercing to depths of thought which perchance no poet has yet adequately expressed. Inasmuch, then, as these sonatas are so wondrously matchless in point of excellence, the violinist need not stint the labour which must be bestowed upon them, in order to gain the power of rendering them effectively and well. She or he may be assured that the time will have been wisely spent in acquiring a mastery over them, and that the toil expended will have been amply repaid, when the longed-for power of playing them has been gained.

(*d*). A variety of selections or picked gems from great works are often thought most desirable. We, however cannot regard many of them as satisfactory in all respects. Although they may be of use in the earlier stages of violin-playing, a tendency which should above all things be avoided may be perchance developed, viz., that of making a cursory, superficial, and most imperfect acquaintance with what is good in music. The greatest works are to be looked upon as indivisible wholes, and certainly do not shine forth in their solemn glory when viewed in isolated portions. A neatly woven garment torn into tatters and glanced at in shreds may still perhaps appear pretty both in colour and design, but it can never be grand or beautiful when viewed in this disjointed state.

INDEX.

A.

	PAGE
Accompaniment	84 to 92
Acoustic Properties of a Building	25
Acoustic Properties of a Violin	30
Advice to the young Amateur	100
Age and Use of Violins	16 to 21
Age not the chief reason of the excellence of the old Violins	16 & 17
Amati, Nicholas,	13, 34, 35, 53
Amati, Andreas,	34
Amati family	34
Amplitude of vibrations	96, 97
Appendix	at end of book
Aristotle's conception of music as the expression of feeling	93
Art of violin-making	30
Astley, Jacob,	91
Auctions, Necessity of careful judgment at,	13 & 14
Auditory apparatus	70 & 93
Authentic tickets	33

B.

Baillot	7
Beat 64, and Appendix	iii
Beethoven's Sonatas 98, and Appendix	iii
Beethoven's words about metronome, Appendix	ii
Bergonzi, Carlo,	39
Blame nowise more necessary than Praise	5
Bow	53 to 56
Bowing	57 to 61
Bowing, Guiseppe Tartini's remarks on	61
Bowing, How much hair should be used in	58
Bowing, Necessity of, in a straight direction,	59
Bowing, Necessity of keeping the bow at the same spot on the strings	59
Bowing should be well performed and without jerks, from the beginning, and also when a note is held out for several bars	60
Bowing should be carefully performed on both strings in double-stopping	60
Bridge, The, of a violin	42 to 44
Broadwood, Collard, and Erard	21 & 22

C.

Carrodus	4
Chanot	45
Classical Music 98, and Appendix	iii
Class-teaching	5
Cleaning of a violin	28
Collard, Broadwood, and Erard	21 & 22
Concluding Remarks	92 to 100
Construction of the Fiddle	30 to 32
Corelli	53 & 100
Cremona	39 & 40

D.

Difficulties, sometimes magnified, sometimes lessened	8
Double-stops, Harmonics, Shifts, and the Shake	79 to 84
Double-stops	79 & 80

INDEX.

E.
Excellence 8
Exercises should be simple at first 6
Ear for music an absolute necessity for good playing but sometimes more easily acquired than the power to play well 9
Erard, Collard, and Broadwood 21 & 22

F.
Fetis, M. 35
Fifth, a perfect . . 63 & 64
Finger-board 46
Fleming, Mr. J. W., . . 32
Forgery and deceit in regard to violins 15
Fork, Tuning, . . 63, 65 & 66
Friendly advice to the young amateur 100

G.
Gagliano, Alessandro, and the Gagliano family . . 38 & 39
Gasparo da Salò of Brescia . 15 & 33
General and Introductory . 1 to 11
General remarks about the violin 29 to 32
Giovanni Paolo Maggini . . 33
Goethe 16
Good violin necessary . 11 to 13
Gradual progress necessary to ensure perfection . . 6
Guarnerius, Andreas . . 35
Guarnerius, Joseph (son of Andrew) 35
Guarnerius, Joseph Antonius 13, 35 & 36
Guarnerius, Pietro, . . 35
Guitar 46

H.
Hair, The, of the bow, . . 54
Harmonics 80
Harmonics how they differ from harmonic upper partial tones of a violin or harp, and the fading harmonics of a piano . 81
Hart, Mr., ... 14
Haweis, The Rev. H. R. . . 15 & 63
Hermann 7
Hill, Mr., . . 14, 28 & 45
History of some Violin-makers . 32 to 40
How to secure a good violin . 13 to 15
Huggins, Mr., . . . 15
Huggins, M., on violin-making of the past and of the future . 20

I.
Importance of buying a good violin . . . . 11 to 13
Instruction books . . 6 & 7
Introductory . . . 1 to 11
Italy, the birthplace of genius . 32

J.
Joachim, Dr., Dedication page & 4 & 69

K.
Kreutzer 7

L.
Labels . . . . 14 & 15
Litolff 7
Loder 7

M.
Manuscript Exercises . . 6
Merits of old Violins, Age and Use . . . . 16 to 22
Metronome. . . Appendix ii
Mozart 25
Mute, The, of a violin . . 45

N.
Nervousness . . 9, 10, 77 & 78
Neruda 4
Noise *versus* power . . 24
Noises *versus* musical sounds . 25

O.
Otto's remarks on the fact that a good violin may sound badly after a long period of disuse . 17

P.
Paganini . . . 3, 32 & 36
Pegs . . . . 44 & 45
Perseverance, Necessity of, . 10 & 11
Perfection must be aimed at Preface & 21
Peters 7
Pianissimo notes of a good violin or good singer very distinctly audible . . . 23, 24 & 25
Pietro Santo Maggini . . 34
Players, Great, . . . 3 & 4
Playing the violin and the teaching of this art contrasted . 4
Playing entirely by ear very wrong 7
Power not opposed to richness of tone 7
Practice . . . . 8 to 11
Preparation of the wood . . 31
Preservation and repair of violins . . . . 26 to 29
Private tuition and class-teaching both necessary . . 5
Progress in playing as years roll on . . . . 10 & 11
Progress in the art of violin-making may in the future be great . . . . 20 & 21
Purchase of a violin . . 10 to 16
Purchase of a violin, summary of important points regarding . 26

INDEX.

R.

Reeves, Mr. William, of 185, Fleet Street, London	7
Resin	45
Rude	7
Rules, Difficulty in observing many at the same time,	67
Rules to be observed in playing	67 to 78
Ruskin	16

S.

Savart's toothed wheel	97
Scales and exercises necessary	6 & 7
Scratching	61
Scoll by Stradivari affixed as part of a fairly good violin very misleading	15
Self-consciousness	9 & 10
Shake	83 & 84
Shift	81 & 82
Sound-bar	40 & 41
Sound-holes	30 & 31
Sound-post	31 & 41
Stainer's violins	97
Stradivari, Antonio,	12, 18, 21, 36, 37, 38 & 53
Stradivari's violins compared with those by Guarnerius	20, 21, & 30
Strauss at the Albert Hall	24
Strings, The. of a violin	46 to 50
Strings. The selection of	49
Stringing, The mode of,	50 to 52
Syren	97

T.

Tartini	54 & 83
Teaching	1 to 5
Teaching and violin-playing contrasted	4
Testing of a violin	21 to 26
The trial of a violin should be carried out in a room provided with furniture and hangings	23
Time	Appendix i, ii, & iii
Tone	85, 94, 97 & 98
Tourte, Francis, of Paris	53
Tours, Berthold	7
Tuning must be performed without that extra twist at the end which one is apt to impart to the peg	66
Tuning must be perfect	62, 63 & 67
Tuning of a violin compared with the tuning of a piano	63
Tuning-fork, The,	63, 65 & 66
Tuning the violin, Mode of,	62 to 67
Tutor	3 & 4
Tyndall, on the good effects produced by playing a violin in regard to an improvement of its tone power	18

U.

Upper Partials	94

V.

Varnish, Secret of best kinds of. for the violin, lost when spirit-varnishes came into general use	19 & 20
Vuillaume of Paris	36 & 53

W.

Wood, preparation of,	18 & 19

CPSIA information can be obtained at www.ICGtesting.com
Printed in the USA
BVOW04s1746221213

339848BV00007B/33/P